the plastic solutions

MARCO SIMEONI
GUNTER PAULI
with JURRIAAN KAMP

The business model that works for the oceans

KAMP SOLUTIONS

KAMP Solutions (English Edition)
525 San Ysidro Rd, Suite D-200,
Montecito CA 93108
Phone: (415) 595-6451
www.kamp.solutions

Ordering Information
Quantity sales. Special discounts are available on quantity purchases by corporations, associations, and others, as well as for college textbook/course adoption use. For details, contact KAMP Solutions at the address above.

Library of Congress Cataloging-in-Publication Data
ISBN: 978-1-7337177-2-4

Cover and interior design: Rick Greer
Production service: Rick Greer

the plastic solutions

MARCO SIMEONI
GUNTER PAULI
with JURRIAAN KAMP

The business model
that works
for the oceans

**KAMP
SOLUTIONS**

Table of Contents

Harnessing the power of business for the common good

By Christopher Wasserman

For decades, business leaders and politicians have been chasing economic growth as the only possible way to provide jobs and better living standards. Great progress has been made. However, in the past twenty years, it has also become clear that people and societies increasingly suffer from the side-effects of this one-dimensional approach —from severe pollution and the destruction of nature to widespread growing inequality and long-term unemployment. We do not seem capable of responding to everyone's needs, including the needs of nature. That's why we started the Zermatt Summit. We wanted to rediscover how business can serve the Common Good.

After the financial crisis of 2008, everyone seemed to think that finance was at the center of the economy and that human beings were basically objects. We want to make sure that we adjust the focus of the economic paradigm from growth and "objects" to well-being and "people". The credo of the Zermatt Summit is that, ultimately, *people* change the world—not *money*. We want to humanize the market economy in general and innovation in particular.

Every year, 2,000 presidents and corporate leaders from around the world get together at the World Economic Forum in Davos. They share a traditional liberal agenda of business and the market economy. In response to the World Economic Forum, a group of non-government organizations (NGOs) launched the World Social Forum in 2001 in Porto Alegre, Brazil. The focus of the World Social Forum is on the needs of people and society. However, the message of the World Social Forum is mostly negative: while it rightly criticizes the status quo, unfortunately it fails to propose concrete alternatives.

In between Davos and Porto Alegre, there is a void that the Zermatt Summit aims to fill. We are a small gathering of some 150 people. We do not criticize from the outside: the Zermatt Summit is a place for insiders—for people who have been in business for many years, who have the means to make a difference, who want to promote necessary change and innovation to serve society, and—most importantly— who walk the talk. That is the huge responsibility of business.

Enterprise is the main economic and social agent in society. But it needs an ethical and humane anchor as our incapacity to provide for drinking water, nutritious food, health care for all, as well as the misuse of private data by a few big corporations, and the trampling of basic human rights have shown. Without awareness and responsibility about and for our actions, society and the whole of humanity can only lose.

Belgium theologian Gérard Fourez said: "Ethics start with the first cry of human suffering".

The Zermatt Summit offers to a committed group of change agents an opportunity to rethink and to renew and to join a community of like-minded leaders. Our vision is that our annual meeting becomes a reference for *human business*—a place where people meet to get inspired, share innovation and together create new business models for a much better world. There is no better proof that our mission is succeeding than this inspiring new book that addresses one of the biggest challenges people, businesses and planet face today.

In 2017, I invited two entrepreneurs and innovators to speak at the Zermatt Summit. Marco Simeoni came to talk about his Race for Water initiative to save the oceans and Gunter Pauli introduced us to his portfolio of Blue Economy projects. That night, after dinner, Marco and Gunter got into a conversation. Marco outlined his vision to use his futuristic boat with solar panels, powered by hydrogen made from seawater, with a kite to sail, and controlled by artificial intelligence to raise awareness about plastic pollution by sailing around the globe. Gunter talked about farming mushrooms on coffee grounds, turning mining waste into paper, and sending data transmission over public streetlights.

The conversation went on for several hours and the two entrepreneurs, in the true spirit of the Zermatt Summit, started to collaborate, literally the next day. They shared a "yes, we can" spirit and bundled their energies, created synergies, and established a joint agenda. A year later, again in Zermatt, Marco and Gunter shared the experience of their collaboration in several initiatives in Peru, Chile, and Rapa Nui. Marco and Gunter had a clear message for the Zermatt Summit and beyond: We will not solve the plastics problem unless we address the economic and social development of the communities that today suffer from the plastic pollution.

This book does not present a "one size fits all" plastic solutions model that can be transplanted around the globe like a franchise chain. Marco and Gunter share the perspective that solutions always blend and change with local needs. However, each solution evolves from a solid business logic that is completely aligned with the mission of the Zermatt Summit: the main reason for business is to serve the Common Good. This book illustrates that Marco and Gunter have made tremendous progress in the past years. I am proud that the book is presented for the first time at the Zermatt Summit.

The Plastic Solutions is a call to join the action. It is the beginning of a movement. This movement needs local enterprise—from the waste collectors who will pick up plastic waste on their bikes in communities around the world to divers fixing the ropes to seed seaweed curtains along coast lines. This movement also needs, as the authors describe in chapter 11, "Captains of Legacy". These are the investors with a multi-generational perspective who are not afraid to make commitments today that they may not see all the benefits from in their own lifetime.

That kind of leadership and vision is what we need today.

Indeed, it resembles the commitment of the cathedral builders of past centuries whose work done over many generations, still inspires millions of people every day. In those days, there were no questions about the amount of the investments made. Building cathedrals was not about efficiencies or cutting corners. *The Plastic Pollutions* presents a $24 billion opportunity. Beyond that opportunity, there are priceless regenerated ecosystems and rebuilt communities. As an entrepreneur, I know, that this is a most meaningful investment. I want to be part of *The Plastic Solutions* and I envision Zermatt as the home of this inspiring movement where we will come together from year to year to strengthen our joint progress as entrepreneurs and investors. This book is proof that the Zermatt Summit succeeds in bringing together the leadership the world needs now. I know it will inspire you as well.

Lausanne, November 2019

Christopher Wasserman is Founder and President of the Zermatt Summit Foundation and President of Terolab Surface Group

An island, plastics and the evolution of science

There are few places on the planet that speak as much to our collective imagination as Rapa Nui, or Easter Island as most of the world has called it for centuries. It is the world's most isolated piece of habitable land. It lies in the Pacific Ocean 3,500 kilometers off the coast of Chile. The nearest habitable island is more than 2,000 kilometers away. Nevertheless, people from Polynesia found their way and, from the 300s, built a flourishing civilization until it mysteriously collapsed.

As hard as it once was for people to get to this remote place, as easy it is today for plastic waste. The beaches of Rapa Nui are full of plastic pollution from faraway places. The once pristine fishing grounds around the island are contaminated with microparticles from anti-aging creams, hair-strengthening agents and more used by consumers thousands of miles away. The plastic pollution on Rapa Nui illustrates the complete failure of the modern consumer society.

It is a failure based on a misunderstanding and misapplication of science. In the same way, we have for the past decades misunderstood the sudden demise of the civilization of Rapa Nui. We based our opinions and judgments on an incomplete understanding of the facts. Today, the progressive understanding of the demise of Rapa Nui offers a great lesson on when we have to change our assumptions and perspectives when we face new facts.

The famous gigantic statues of Rapa Nui suggest an advanced civilization capable of moving pieces of rock up to 20 meters high and weighing more than 200 tons. We also know that, in just a few centuries, the civilization of Rapa Nui almost completely disappeared. The islanders appeared to have wiped out their forests and driven their plants and animals to extinction. They destroyed their statues and even appear to have descended into cannibalism to survive. What happened? And why?

The mystery of Rapa Nui has fascinated researchers and scientists for decades. In the 1940s, Thor Heyerdahl visited the island with his notorious Kon-Tiki raft to prove that people from South America could have settled Polynesia in pre-Columbian times. In the 1990s various paleontologists did thorough excavations and studies on Rapa Nui. Using the newly developed techniques of pollen analysis and carbon dating, they established that trees, bushes, grasses, flowers, fruits and herbs once grew in abundance on the island. However, Dutch explorer Jacob Roggeveen noted in 1722 that the island's "wasted appearance could give no other impression than of a singular poverty and barrenness". Roggeveen, who was supposed to find *Terra Australis* (Australia) but instead became the first European visitor to land on the island on Easter, April 5th that year, and he gave the name foreigners have used for centuries.

Pollen records show the destruction of forests on Rapa Nui was well under way by the year 800. In other words, only some 500 years after the beginning of human settlement and long before the arrival of Roggeveen. The records show rats, that came in the boats with the first Polynesian settlers, multiplied in abundance and became a plague. The scientists discovered that the rats ate the nuts of the native palm tree, a primary source of food for the local population, preventing its regeneration. Their analysis established a picture of one of the most extreme examples of forest destruction anywhere in the world.

From there, the scientists made quick leaps forward and built a damning hypothesis: The Rapa Nuiers had committed the first *ecocide*, a criminal attempt to carelessly destroy the ecosystem that provided for their own health and well-being. In combination with the anecdotes of apparent cannibalism, the story of Rapa Nui became a warning sign for our modern society that is also very much on a collision course with nature. Perhaps one day, the skyscrapers of Manhattan will stand deserted like the statues of Rapa Nui? This is the apocalyptic message of the book *Collapse* by Jared Diamond that is part of the curriculum of many environmental courses around the world.

Stories are powerful. Today, tourists visiting Rapa Nui shake their heads looking at the statues while thinking about the shortsightedness of humans who didn't seem able to preserve life for generations to come. The islanders can hardly escape a sense of shame for the carelessness of their ancestors.

But the story is not true. The population of Rapa Nui did not commit ecocide. We had to wait until the 21st century when the human genome was declared complete and it became possible to analyze the movement of populations in a completely new way. The new DNA science showed Polynesian genes from Rapa Nuiers in the population of Peru and other South American nations. This gene flow happened before the arrival of the European traders. The DNA evidence points to a different explanation. Perhaps the inhabitants of Rapa Nui were victims of South American slave raids and the pretended cannibalism was used as an excuse to subdue the whole population. They should not be blamed for their self-destruction!

The point is that science evolves, and as science changes, stories change. Rapa Nui was once invaded by rats. Today, the island is invaded by plastics from faraway places. Let us be clear: the discovery of plastic was once a tremendous achievement. The flexibility of the material made life easier in many ways. In a way, the invention of plastics created the modern consumer. Plastic was a great story. Until it showed up on the beaches of distant Rapa Nui. Until it was everywhere. Until we began to realize that plastic pollution threatens the foundation of life. The much-celebrated inventors of plastics, today, look like the ancestors on Rapa Nui, who didn't understand that the rats were eating the roots and seeds of the palm trees that provided their food and maintained their future. How could these plastic innovators NOT design a product that would decompose and degrade in sun, sea and soil and would never cause pollution for centuries to come?

The bad story of plastic can come to a happy ending. Science continues to advance and allows entrepreneurs, who want to contribute to the Common Good, to change the story again. As it turns out, science has a way of cleaning up the plastic pollution on Rapa Nui. Science can recover the molecules that constitute today's plastics and transform them into something new, useful and clean.

In fact, if we focus our efforts on understanding how nature works, we can help nature to clean up the plastic microparticles in the oceans. And science can create plastics that are in harmony with the cycles of nature, where the waste of one is nutrition or energy for the other. It cannot be that humans are the only species on earth capable of producing millions of tons of something that no one else desires or needs after a single use! The first plastic solutions are there; more will emerge as investors and entrepreneurs embrace the historic opportunities to correct some monumental mistakes of the past. It may take decades, even a century, but with time, Rapa Nui can become a pristine paradise again.

A new and better plastics story is emerging. That is the story of this book.

Photo: © Copyright August 2019, Peter Charaf. R4WO Plastic mismanagement in Filipino community on Gaya Island Borneo.

Photo: © Copyright Peter Charaf

A plastic solutions movement

Have you ever eaten a credit card?

"No!", you'll say.

But, more than likely, you have.

In fact, you probably eat a credit card each week.

The average human ingests some five grams of plastic every week. That's the total weight of the microplastics you consume that come with the bottled water, the plastic lettuce box, the wrapped cucumber you buy or the fish you eat in a restaurant. Five grams of plastic each week. That's the weight of a credit card.

Most people are aware that plastic pollution is a problem. We have seen pictures of plastic-covered beaches that look like landfills and of fish hopelessly caught in plastic waste. We have seen a straw being pulled out of the nostrils of a turtle. And who has not been shocked by the image of a plastic cord cutting through the neck of a sea lion? Between five and ten percent of all plastics end up in the oceans.

Plastic pollution has turned the oceans into the largest waste dumps on the planet. Yes, we are becoming aware and we read about—so far, mostly unsuccessful—attempts to clean up the oceans. However, did we forget that salt is a preservation agent? So, plastics—even most of the biodegradable ones—will never break down in saltwater, but only wither down into tiny pieces, the infamous microplastics that cannot yet be collected by manmade technologies.

Most people do not yet realize that plastic not only pollutes the land and the seas around us. Plastic has entered the very food chain that our lives depend on. We ingest more than 100,000 plastic micro particles annually—the weight of a credit card each week. The micro particles are in the fish we eat. The water bottles we use leak plastic particles too. Canadian researchers recently showed that steeping a single plastic layered tea bag releases about 11.6 million miniscule plastic microparticles and 3.1 billion "nanoplastics" in your teacup—the smaller the particles, the easier they can enter the organs in our bodies. Note: industry added that plastic layer some years ago to prevent that the paper tea bag easily fell apart. In other words: industry took care of the bag, not of the consumer.

Plastic is everywhere. Even in the Arctic, microscopic particles of plastic are falling out of the sky with snow, a recent study has found. Studies show that three to seven percent of the fine particles in the air come from dust caused by the tires of the millions of the cars on the roads. An average home accumulates some 20 kilograms of dust per year—30 percent of that is plastic. We know that plastic contains lots of toxic ingredients. We do not know yet what the impact of that hazardous consumption will be on our health because current science is not yet able to study the smallest particles. We have started a dangerous experiment with life, and the statistics before us forebode no good news. We are increasingly aware. We realize that our best efforts are a mere drop in the bucket, and we have no clue what to do.

We leave it to politicians who are not or insufficiently acting. Their efforts are focused on banning or taxing practices and products, but they do not lead to constructing new realities. We are hoping that scientists come up with a breakthrough solution that will change the dark reality once and for all. We desperately need solutions and we need to roll them out with speed and scale.

The point is we need plastics. We should not forget that plastics give a big improvement to our quality of life. It is hard to imagine hospitals with secure sanitation without single use plastics. What about windmills—that produce clean energy—, and lighter cars and aircraft—that are more fuel-efficient—without plastics? Plastic has great performances. The problem is that, in most cases, we only use it for a very short time and then we throw it away causing widespread pollution. Forty percent of the annual plastics production that is responsible for 80 percent of the plastic pollution in the oceans, is used for packaging… There is a major disconnect between the use of a plastic and its actual impact on the quality of life. How can we have ever allowed the use of a water bottle that needs hundreds of years to decompose while it functions in our daily lives for less than an hour?

Every second 20,000 new plastic bottles are produced around the world. Global plastic production has crossed 400 million tons per year and is scheduled to hit one billion tons per year in the next 25 years. This is a trend that—despite the admirable initiatives of queens, prime ministers and progressive businesses—can hardly be stopped.

However, we can change the role of plastics in our societies. We can redesign the ways we produce and consume plastics. The supply chain from raw material to handling the end of life of any polymer must include more value, much more at every step along the way. As we shall see in this book, with a better business model that is not based on a single solution but rather on a portfolio of locally adapted approaches, we can both stop the pollution and clean up the mess. In the process, we can even lift millions out of poverty.

Introducing new profitable business models is the work of entrepreneurs. That's why this book is written by entrepreneurs. Plastic pollution is a problem that was created by business ever driving for more savings, lower costs, better margins and higher performance. This model causes social and environmental stress and is only producing financial returns for shareholders. Therefore, a new competitive model that responds to the needs of all in ways much better than today's plastics ever did, can only be successfully introduced by business too. Non-profit initiatives can raise awareness, but they can never develop and maintain long-term, ongoing, sustainable solutions that create multiple benefits—

including solid financial returns—while putting nature back on its evolutionary path. The challenge is that very few entrepreneurs are dedicating their creativity and energy to solving the plastic problem while designing business models that transform reality. Until now.

In the past 25 years, we have worked on business solutions for plastic pollution. We have worked with engineers and scientists to discover new ways of adding value to plastic waste. We have found ways to truly regenerate the oceans—including, most importantly, the cleaning up of the microparticles that we can hardly see but that are everywhere. If we add some smart policy changes; teaching each aspiring chemical engineer how to design polymers that degrade in sun, sea and soil, plastic pollution will become a thing of the past while plastics will remain part of our future. It is going to take time. A lot of time. It may take a hundred years, or even longer, before the oceans are free of plastic again. But the message of this book is that we can do the good work of stopping and cleaning up the pollution while we are supporting livelihoods. Smart investors are going to make money solving the problem. And we know from abundant historic examples that profitable systems work!

This book presents a business model to transform the role of plastics in society and the people behind it. The first chapter introduces Marco Simeoni as the Swiss tech entrepreneur and passionate sailor who started the Race for Water Foundation and discovered that we won't be able to clean up the oceans with clever modern manmade technology. You'll learn what he did next.

The second chapter introduces Gunter Pauli as the founder of a global network of scientists and entrepreneurs that is focused on building businesses that are regenerating nature and rebuilding communities. From that focus an integrated systemic solution for plastic pollution arises.

In the third chapter we evaluate the current solutions that despite passion and wisdom, so far, have not changed the tide. We look into recycling, alternative resources, public policy, cleanup initiatives, and more. We find what is missing: a business model that attributes commercial value to all plastic waste without the need for taxation—a business model based on the logic of nature, cascading nutrients, energy and matter producing always better outcomes supporting the common good.

In the fourth chapter we tell the story of the Race for Water boat and its scientific and educational mission. We explain how the boat is showing communities around the world a pathway to clean energy independence. In chapter 5 we lay down the principles for the production and consumption of plastics that are not just focused on protection of the environment but also on the regeneration of nature through a circular economy. In chapter 6 we analyze how humanity is undermining its own future through depriving itself of the value of waste. We present how a circular strategy, that begins with diapers, can replenish the soil.

Our understandable need to prevent fire in our daily lives has led to the addition of many toxic substances to plastics. In chapter 7 we show how these chemical cocktails can be replaced with healthy, cheaper, and effective natural alternatives. Chapter 8 presents a breakthrough solution to immediately address and stop 80 percent of the plastic pollution. In chapter 9 we show how we can engage nature to begin cleaning up the oceans. In chapter 10, we present the comprehensive new business model that mimics nature and combines different technologies to stop the dumping of toxic plastic waste and begin the cleaning and regeneration of the oceans. This model is not a final blueprint for one global solution but rather a first phase business approach which determines the trajectory. The final chapter introduces investors to a legacy opportunity to serve future generations.

There is one essential element at the core of our plastics strategy. Throughout the book, we present practical small-scale solutions that do not require a lot of capital and that can quickly be replicated and scaled around the world. This is not the work of one big global corporation. And, yet, this is a gigantic global effort. It is an opportunity for millions of people to participate, create jobs and support communities.

There is a famous scene in the movie *The Graduate* made in 1967 when the plastics revolution was only beginning. The Dustin Hoffman character is a young college student searching for a meaningful future. A visiting family friend takes a moment to give him some career advice. "I want to say one word to you", he says. As the young student listens intently, the man says: "Plastics…. there is a great future in plastics".

The scene is full of irony as the plastics industry is about the last thing the idealistic graduate would consider.

However, half a century later the message rings true. There is indeed a great future in plastics—new and very different plastics that serve people and society. We are starting a global plastic solutions movement that you, and anyone, can join. That's why you want to read this book now.

Get inspired, enjoy, and act!

Chapter 1

Marco Simeoni: An unlikely environmental activist

I saw the solution for plastic pollution when, one evening, I was having a beer outside a café in Rio de Janeiro.

It was a warm tropical night. While I was listening to music, I noticed that a man was watching me. At a polite distance, he seemed to be waiting for something. When I finished my beer, he came to me and asked for my can. The aluminum had so much value for him that it was worth for him to wait for me to finish my beer.

That night I learned a critical lesson that lies at the core of my solution for plastic pollution. Aluminum waste has value. People make a living recycling it. In Rio alone, there are more than 150,000 people recycling aluminum. Plastic waste, on the other hand, has no value. That's why plastic is polluting the environment, the oceans, and our lives. The solution to the plastic problem has to begin with finding a value for plastic waste.

But, first, let me tell you my story. I didn't come into this life as an environmental activist. I grew up close to Lausanne in Switzerland. Beautiful nature was around me and I often played in the nearby forest. But at home we didn't talk much about environmental issues. My relationship with nature changed, when I fell in love with sailing. In Switzerland, we have many beautiful lakes. I loved the freedom of sailing, and the connection with the forces of nature: sun, wind and water.

Freedom has always been very important to me. I do not like working for a boss or people telling me what to do. So, I was bound to become an entrepreneur. I like to solve problems. For me it always starts with a blank page and then I begin to imagine the solution. When the solution comes off the ground and becomes a running business, my job is done. I'm not good at managing processes and keeping a company running. Then I need to move on to the next challenge.

I decided to become a computer engineer in the 1980s when the desktop computer was being introduced. I was excited about the new technology and I wanted to fully understand the potential. There were lots of challenges to be met. I saw an opportunity to connect the possibilities of the new desktop with the main frame computers that—at that time—were still running processes with proprietary software. There was a need to build these connections and to develop bridges between those two different worlds. In 1995, that was the focus of my first IT consulting company. I was the first one doing this in Switzerland. I hired people from the mainframe computer world and people who knew about the new desktops and I brought them together to develop interconnection—gateway—solutions. Subsequently, with my associates, we started several more companies to cover most of the IT portfolio. Ultimately, we brought the companies together in a holding company, the Veltigroup. In 2015, I sold the Veltigroup to the Swiss telecommunications provider, Swisscom.

While I was building companies, sailing always remained an important part of my life. After I got my offshore license, I increasingly began to sail the oceans. The experience of nature is even more abundant on the seas. However, I also began to discover that there was always garbage floating around the boat. One day my entrepreneurial gene kicked in and I could no longer continue watching the pollution in the ocean and do nothing. That's when, in 2010, I started the Race for Water Foundation. My original objective was to raise awareness for the need to preserve the oceans through a sailboat race—a race to preserve water.

With my associates, Swiss professional offshore sailor, Steve Ravussin, and French windsurfer and 1992 Barcelona Olympic gold medalist, Franck David, we had a special plan for that race. The outcome of most sailing races depends a lot on the quality and the technology of the boats. We decided to build one standard boat—the Multi One Design 70 (MOD 70, for 70 feet). Every boat would be exactly the same. So, not the best boat but the best team would win. We built seven multihull boats and organized several races. Then we hit the European financial crisis of 2012 and we lost many of our sponsors. We had to discontinue organizing the race, but I kept the first boat.

In 2015, after I had sold my company, I decided to go on an expedition with my first boat which I had named "Race for Water". In these days, I was talking a lot about the plastic pollution in the ocean, but I realized that I really didn't know much about the problem. I was reading in newspapers about five major gyres—islands—of plastic in the oceans and I wanted to see that for myself. That year, I sailed all the oceans. However, I never saw "islands" of plastic.

I saw plastic soup. I discovered that a lot of plastic sinks, and what does not sink breaks down in small pieces. I saw microparticles everywhere. No matter where you are on the oceans and how far from the coast, if you look through binoculars around your boat for a while, you will see plastic. I learned that only some three percent of the plastic waste is floating, and I quickly realized that people can't clean the oceans. I'm a sailor. I know that you can have 15 meters high waves in the middle of the ocean. There are winds that blow more than 100 kilometers an hour. Some of the seas are thousands of meters deep.

I had my own terrifying experience with the mighty forces of the oceans. In the middle of the Indian Ocean—close to the atoll Diego Garcia, known for its secretive US and British naval and military bases—our catamaran capsized. You can't turn back a catamaran. We had to wait for help. Luckily, we all survived, and we were able to use our satellite phone to ask for help. We drifted at sea for two and a half days before the British navy was able to rescue us.

It was a stressful experience and I realized very well that I was risking my life to understand how big the problem of plastic pollution is. Drifting at sea and feeling very vulnerable, you realize that the ocean is not a swimming pool that can be cleaned with a robot as some have proposed. Oceans cover 70 percent of the planet. There is no way we can clean that with manmade structures. However, nature can do it as we will discover later in this book.

We need to stop the plastic pollution reaching the oceans. Our efforts should be focused on land before the plastics reach the water. And that's critical: Today every minute the equivalent of a garbage truck load of plastic is dumped in the ocean. If nothing is done, there will more plastic than fish in the oceans by 2050. More than 25 percent of the fish already have toxic plastic in their stomachs and livers. That is a health disaster waiting to happen as half of humanity is dependent on seafood for their daily diet. Our own liver is accumulating plastics faster than we ever realized slowly mummifying our body!

My plastic odyssey brought me to the places on land where the pollution is worst. I visited Kamilo beach on the Big Island of Hawaii which gets buried in plastics again and again. It is like walking on a landfill. None of that plastic is local; it all comes from the sea. The local population organizes beach cleanups only to do it again and again. I visited Easter Island, which lies in the middle of nowhere: 3,500 kilometers of the coast of Chile and 4,000 kilometers from Polynesia. And yet, every year 50 tons of plastics ends on the beaches there. It keeps coming. It never stops. I met children in slums who only know a world full of plastic waste around them, who do not know the beauty of undisturbed nature.

I saw terrible plastic pollution in cities in Asia and Latin America. I learned the hopeless facts. Packaging material that we maybe use for 20 minutes, takes 400 years to disintegrate.

There are seven families of plastic that cannot be recycled together, and the industry keeps adding additives to improve the performance of plastics. Many of these additives are toxic but nobody knows exactly which ingredients are used and where. I read the study that calculates that plastic pollution reduces the natural capital of the oceans with $2.5 trillion a year—not even counting the impact on human health. Nobody is paying for that destruction of vital, life-supporting natural capital.

There is probably only one statistic that gives me hope. As it turns out, 80 percent of the plastic waste comes from low-income countries. It comes from countries where trash collection and recycling hardly exist. We know that, in these same countries, lots of people are making a living recycling other waste from paper to aluminum and much more. There is no pollution from waste that has value. These informal trash collectors do not collect plastic because it has no value. That brings me back to my experience in Rio and a core strategic reflection: If we can offer these trash collectors a fee that makes collecting plastic as attractive as collecting aluminum cans, these people can stop the plastic pollution while they improve their own lives. That's the kind of problem I knew I could solve.

Chapter 2

Gunter Pauli: A green entrepreneur with a new business model

In the late 1980s, as a young man, I got the opportunity to publish European languages editions of the annual "State of the World" report by Lester Brown's Worldwatch Institute, the international environmental thinktank based in Washington D.C. Brown was ahead of his time. He documented early on that humanity was on a collision course with the very ecosystem that supports all life.

As the European publisher of the reports, I felt honored to be involved with such important work. And yet, the ongoing stream of negative analyses about the environment also depressed me. I wanted to contribute. I wanted to make things better. I was too young to see the world go down in pollution and degradation.

I was soon presented with a new opportunity. As publisher of the annual reports of the Worldwatch Institute, I had become an environmental expert in my native Belgium. I had been invited to join the board of a small green detergent company, and I had gladly accepted because I knew the problems with soaps. I had read the reports that ever more powerful soaps that only degraded in sewage systems weeks after they had been discharged, destroyed marine life in rivers. These cleaning products would wash fish for months after they had removed a stain from a shirt. It was about time for a new vision for biodegradable soap.

In the beginning of the 1990s, I became CEO and co-owner of this Belgian ecological cleaning products manufacturer, Ecover. I was proudly spreading the word that our company was a pioneer of biodegradable soaps. But then, I learned a critical lesson about sustainability.

I discovered that rainforests in Indonesia were being cut to create plantations to produce the palm oil that was a key ingredient of our detergents. I thought we were doing it perfectly. Ecover was 100 percent biodegradable—that was 99.9 percent better than the competition. Unfortunately, while we were cleaning rivers in Europe, we were destroying rainforests and the habitat of orangutans in Asia. We had designed a business model that turns rainforests into palm plantations for the sake of money. When I couldn't convince my partner that success for Ecover would come from even better soap which would not destroy rainforests, and not from lower costs, I left the company. Today, I see the same conflict in the lack of progress in addressing plastic pollution. That pollution is the result of the business model that we have created. The business model is the problem. So, the solution must be in the design of a *better* business model.

Waste and pollution—but also global warming and poverty—are caused by the narrow-minded focus on the "core business" and "economies of scale". In the world of globalization, you have to produce more of the same at the lowest possible cost. Thus, you standardize and robotize, drive down costs, and steal from the planet wherever it is permitted. In a business model that is only based on cutting costs, the entrepreneur is forced to cut corners and to make abstractions of the impact of his business on the life that supports us all.

When you only see one-dimensional relationship between costs and profit, there is no place for a focus on generating value wherever you can to respond to the basic needs of all. Business should not be focused on minimizing its negative impact on the environment. That's not enough. Stealing less is still stealing; polluting less is still polluting. Certified monoculture forest plantations still disrupt ecosystems and decimate biodiversity. The overriding objective should be to always do more good. In fact, the only focus every entrepreneur always has to have is to find the ways to serve society and the needs of people best, and to maintain nature on its evolutionary path. That's the single reason for the existence of a business. When that's clear, the relationship with—for instance—plastics immediately changes. You are not going to use plastics that last for hundreds of years only once, and then throw them in a bin, passing on the responsibility to deal with it to others while squandering fossil fuel resources.

We live in an economic logic wherein we ship butter, sugar, palm oil, eggs, milk and dried fruits around the globe to bake cookies that are also shipped around the world so that we can have cookies with the same taste whenever and wherever we desire, at whatever cost. At each stage of the transformation

35

we use plastics for packaging, and each time we mostly use it once—briefly. Such an oversimplified approach to production in ever-higher volumes has led to a world of hunger and pollution amidst plenty.

We celebrate Adam Smith as the father of the market economy based on efficient production and trade. However, his "invisible hand" has been a disaster for the air we breathe, for the biodiversity that feeds us, and for the water we drink. In the markets, the invisible hand may have stimulated efficiencies of supply and demand, but the so-called enlightened self-interest of the manufacturer also means that every polluter knows that each little additional bit of pollution they add, is shared by everyone—they do not pay the price themselves; *everyone* pays.

I have studied this phenomenon for three decades. After the Earth Summit in Rio de Janeiro in 1992, at the request of the Japanese government and in cooperation with the United Nations University, I set up *Zero Emissions Research and Initiatives* (ZERI). This has become a global network of 3,000 scientists and entrepreneurs focused on creating, what I call, a "Blue Economy". Because "green" is simply not good enough. With the "reduce, reuse, recycle" mantra we can't end the destruction. We have to stop. That means zero. We do not accept a factory where routinely 0.5 percent of the workers get involved in accidents. The only acceptable objective is: zero accidents, or TQM (total quality management). That's the only adequate target for the environment as well.

I propose a business model that is completely geared towards generating as much *value* as possible with whatever is locally available. All business should be focused on regenerating ecosystems including social and economic communities. My favorite example is coffee, the world's second-most traded commodity after oil. Most people who drink coffee every day do not realize that they only ingest 0.2 percent of the coffee cherry, 99.8 percent of the bean is wasted. First the peel—the world's richest source of antioxidants—is thrown away and subsequently we discard the grounds after the coffee is brewed. At best, we are composting. But that does not make any sense. How can farmers thrive when the business model only values a tiny fraction of their produce? However, in that injustice also lies the opportunity. If only 0.2 percent of the coffee bean is used, we can theoretically do 500 times better. Once you realize that you can go from 0.2 percent to 100 percent use of material, you can generate economic growth and respond to the needs of people.

My coffee cycle begins with the coffee grounds. They provide an ideal substrate for farming mushrooms. Mushrooms can be sold to humans and the leftovers can be fed to chickens that will give eggs. We do not have to ask the Earth to do more for us; we can do so much more with what the planet is already generously providing.

It works. Since we first introduced this coffee model to a group of orphans in Zimbabwe twenty years ago, the experiment has been successfully replicated in some 5,000 communities around the world. In these communities, hunger and poverty have been overcome simply by using free available waste—coffee grounds but also green waste from food crops—to produce food (mushrooms). With a focus to respond to local needs with what is locally available, you can perfectly outcompete the globalization model. But take note: by definition, the new business model leads to different outcomes and results in different places. Giving waste value and using what you already have, you learn to do much more to respond to everyone's needs without asking nature to do more—without exploiting nature.

A recent invention takes the coffee story to a new dimension: Coffee Pixels, a startup in Latvia, has introduced a solid bar made from the whole coffee bean. The coffee cherry has a peel rich in nutrition. Ten grams of the bar has 50 milligrams of caffeine, about as much as in an expresso or a can of Red Bull for which people pay $2 or more. The economic opportunity is potentially far-reaching. With a ton of coffee, a farmer can produce more value than any organic, fair trade or shade grown initiative has ever imagined. Coffee bars can be sold at half the price of Red Bull but with the same amount of caffeine. That means that a ton of coffee can generate an income of $100,000. Today, a coffee farmer gets $600 for a ton, or perhaps $800 if the coffee is organic and fair trade. In other words: If you give value to 100 percent of the coffee bean, you are going to change lives.

Here's another example of creating value that touches the plastics challenge. A life cycle assessment once concluded that—from an environmental perspective—given weight and distribution, it makes more sense to use plastic bottles than glass ones. That conclusion comes from the same linear thinking that drives the core business concept. Nature, however, never uses something only once. Nature never recycles a product directly into the same product. No tree tries to *recycle* its leaves, keeping the foliage from the autumn to be re-attached in the spring. Instead, a tree drops its leaves which are converted through armies of species including earthworms, ants, fungi, micro-organisms into humus which feeds the tree again through the roots, blended with rain and bird poop. And everyone contributes to the process that is never ending.

Just like it does not make sense for the tree to recycle its leaves, it does not make sense to turn glass bottles into glass bottles. Glass bottles are better converted into glass foam blended with CO_2 as bubbles. That's a superior insulation product. Turning glass bottles into insulation material means adding value. An insulation material made from wasted bottles that resists acids, water—no mold ever grows on it—and even keeps rats at bay provides quite a different perspective than we get from a life cycle assessment.

Glass foam can be recycled forever, and it does not burn, and therefore does not need the flame-retardant chemicals that are suspected to cause cancer (see chapter 7). It can hardly get better. In this business model, it does not make any sense anymore to use plastic bottles. It becomes absurd to continue using plastic bottles, even with the label "biodegradable"— which, we will learn, is not the same as "biodegraded".

We know that it makes business sense to build a glass insulation factory when you can feed that factory with 5.5 million glass bottles a year—given current glass consumption you need a town of about 40,000 people for that volume. That means you can reduce energy wasted in houses using locally produced insulation material made from locally used glass bottles and create a healthier living environment.

To change the business model, we have to ask the question: "How does nature do it?". Nature has an incredibly efficient business model. There is no waste in nature, no pollution, and no unemployment. Nature's design principles provide remarkable solutions for complex problems and continually increasing diversity to build up resilience against unexpected disturbances. Nature self-regulates climate, decontamination and mineralization of water, and conversion of residues into food. Nature prevents erosion, maintains soil fertility, pollinates, and balances pests and populations. It maintains life cycles and genetic diversity at productivity levels far beyond any human-made technology. Aircrafts are clumsy structures compared with the efficiency of hummingbirds. And there is no stronger material than the silk of a spider.

In my vision, ending plastic pollution becomes an obvious result of a new business model based on natural principles. We should not fight waste but completely eliminate the concept of waste. The overriding ethical objective should be to do more good—for people and planet. It is simply the best business strategy: the more good you can do, the more competitive—and successful—you are. Clients will be loyal and reward you with repeat sales. In any environment, we can turn this logic into a portfolio of opportunities, provided by and in line with nature. Once you have discovered this amazing cluster of opportunities, we must inspire people to act. And, then we say: "By the way: it is zero emissions and zero waste". That's it. End of discussion.

Chapter 3
The need for intelligent design

It is a familiar scene. Someone is holding the plastic leftovers of a meal or an empty drink bottle while standing in front of a few recycle containers studying the pictures explaining what to put in which container. Ultimately, the recycling-conscious citizen gives up and dumps his trash in one of the containers. Other people do not even look at the confusing pictograms anymore and just throw their stuff in a container hoping it is the right one.

Recycling should be an essential component of any successful strategy to stop the plastic pollution. However, the reality is that most consumers have no clue about the details of plastic recycling. Many are suspicious about what happens with these recycling containers. Rightly so. Today, in the advanced nations of the world that have suitable trash collection infrastructures only a fraction of all plastics—less than ten percent—is properly recycled. The bulk of used plastics is burned or, even worse, dumped in landfills. In the United States, more than 90 percent of the plastic waste ends up in landfills where it will pollute soil and groundwater for centuries to come.

Or, western countries export their problem and send their plastic waste to less-developed countries. For years, China was the main receiver of plastic pollution from other countries. Forty-five percent of the world's plastic waste was sold to China despite the fact that the country had no infrastructure to effectively process it. In 2017, China ended the despicable practice. That year, the US as the world's top exporter of plastic waste, sent almost one million tons to China. After the Chinese closed their borders and disrupted the flow of more than seven million tons of plastic trash a year, Malaysia became the main destination for the world's plastic pollution. However, in 2019, Malaysia also began rejecting rich countries' rubbish, sending containers back.

The impact was predictable. After the Asian countries began closing their borders, the largest recycling company in California was forced to close as there is no more market to sell the plastics to. Most of that exported plastic pollution was never recycled anyway, but—for lack of a better infrastructure—simply burned releasing carbon emissions and toxic gases far away from the wealthy consumers who created it. Meanwhile, the positive effect of China's new policy is that plastic recycling rates in that country are shooting up. Plastic recycling in China increased with 11 percent in 2017, the year the country banned the import of plastic waste. China's plastics recycling rate is now 22 percent, more than double the rate in the US. China is using the supply void resulting from the import ban to process its own waste. Official Chinese estimates put the value of the recycling industry at $ 1 trillion and the sector could provide 40 million new jobs by 2030.

These numbers make clear that recycling is a strategic priority for any country.

Nonetheless, the policy changes in China and Malaysia only highlight the failure of the current global plastics recycling system. The point is that it is relatively easy to make new paper from wastepaper, or new aluminum from used aluminum. We can turn old car tires into new ones and use the chemicals of old batteries for new batteries. Plastic recycling, however, is complex and difficult. To begin with, there are six different "families" of plastics and a seventh category for all the plastics that do not fit in any of the six main categories. Different plastics cannot be recycled together. That simply means that one empty container in the wrong recycling bin renders the whole recycling effort futile. At present, recycling only truly works for two varieties—high density polyethylene (HDPE) and polypropylene (PET)—because the recycled material can more or less compete with virgin material. Some plastics are theoretically recyclable, but it is not economical, and it does not happen despite the infamous triangle on the plastic materials.

Many plastic products contain various layers of different plastics, metals and even paper creating inseparable mixes. Engineers excel in putting things together for easy mass production, but no engineer has a clue how to take these things apart again. Often, it is not even clear (anymore) to which family a particular piece of plastic belongs.

Even industry experts or professional recyclers may end up in the same desperate situation as the well-meaning consumer standing in front of the recycle bins. The market forces are

The Plastic Solutions

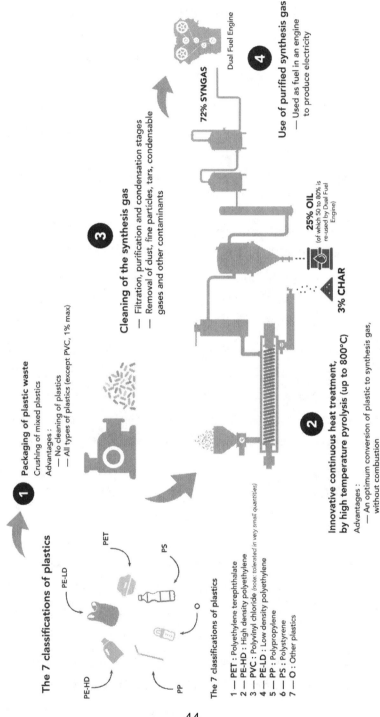

The 7 classifications of plastics

PE-LD

PET

PS

PE-HD

PP

O

The 7 classifications of plastics

1 — PET : Polyethylene terephthalate
2 — PE-HD : High density polyethylene
3 — PVC : Polyvinyl chloride (note: tolerated in very small quantities)
4 — PE-LD : Low density polyethylene
5 — PP : Polypropylene
6 — PS : Polystyrene
7 — O : Other plastics

1 **Packaging of plastic waste**
Crushing of mixed plastics
Advantages :
— No cleaning of plastics
— All types of plastics (except PVC, 1% max)

2 **Innovative continuous heat treatment, by high temperature pyrolysis (up to 800°C)**
Advantages :
— An optimum conversion of plastic to synthesis gas, without combustion

3 **Cleaning of the synthesis gas**
— Filtration, purification and condensation stages
— Removal of dust, fine particles, tars, condensable gases and other contaminants

3% CHAR

25% OIL
(of which 50 to 80% is re-used by Dual Fuel Engine)

72% SYNGAS

Dual Fuel Engine

4 **Use of purified synthesis gas**
— Used as fuel in an engine to produce electricity

simply not capable of dealing with the vast majority of complex plastic types. Just imagine the job for a well-meaning manager of an nvironmentally conscious store or hotel who wants to stop the use of all plastics…

Moreover, many plastics contain highly toxic additives to improve their usability. Plastic toys, for instance, may contain flame retardants because we want our children to be safe. Other plastics contain phthalates that make them soft. There are UV blockers to extend the life of plastics. There is Bisphenol A (BPA) that has been banned after a long legal battle but that still shows up in the old plastics floating in the oceans. Many of these additives have been recognized as trade secrets and do not need to be disclosed. That means that we are consuming chemical cocktails without any knowledge or understanding of the health risks or how these additives can be removed during recycling.

The known poisonous and carcinogenic substances need to be removed to be able to turn waste plastic in usable new raw material. It may sound great to wear shoes, or even a sweater, made from plastic recovered from the oceans. But to which harmful chemicals are you exposing your body? As a result, even in the most advanced places, we are nowhere near an effective and economical recycling structure for plastics. Who wants to take the health risk?

There are initiatives to skip the proper recycling efforts and turn the whole plastic "soup" into new plastic products—from art objects to furniture and from fishing nets to even new roads. Net-Works is an initiative that pays fishermen in the Philippines and Cameroon to recover discarded fishing nets from the ocean. The nets are subsequently sold to businesses that turn them into products. Since 2013, fishermen have collected 224 tons of fishing nets. This has provided new income to 2,200 families. Bureo in Chile is an initiative, supported by US green outdoor clothing pioneer Patagonia, that turns fishing nets into skateboards and sunglasses. Healthy Seas removes plastic waste from the seas. The waste is transformed into a yarn that is basis for new products, such as socks, swimwear or carpets.

Aquafil Group is a leading international player in the production of recycled fibres and polymers, primarily Nylon 6, Dryarn and XLA, but also, more recently, it is the inventor and only producer of ECONYL, a polyamide made from 100% recycled raw materials. These materials include post-consumer fishing nets, carpets, clothing, rugs, and rigid textiles, as well as pre-consumer waste like oligomers and scraps generated by the production of Nylon 6. Brands like Ecoalf that go under the slogan "Because there is no Planet B" heavily rely on Aquafil for their successful marketing campaigns.

These are admirable initiatives. But given the presence of the same additives we just talked about, these new products, and their manufacturing, may very well be very dangerous and unhealthy. Companies in Asia are making toys (!) from recycled plastics that contain ten times the accepted norm of bromine flame retardants. The mechanical recycling does not remove these toxins.

Formally, the plastics industry supports recycling. In 2013 in the United States, the American Chemistry Council launched the Wrap Recycling Action Program (WRAP). The program works with local and state governments, and retailers to educate consumers about what types of plastic film are recyclable, and how and where to recycle it. Similarly, the Plastics Industry Association, a lobby group that includes multinationals like Shell, Exxon Mobil, Chevron Phillips and Dow Dupont that have vast plastics interests, launched A Bag's Life as a program to promote recycling of plastic bags. What is less known, is that the same lobby group actively campaigns in U.S. states to block bans of plastic bags and other single-use plastic products. In the state of Tennessee, for instance, such a preemption bill passed the state legislature. It means that local governments in the state cannot pass any bans on plastics anymore. The industry support for recycling becomes window dressing for contemptuous attempts to protect the interests of the small group of shareholders of the companies that produce the plastics.

Recycling remains a major challenge, even if it is possible to get rid of toxic additives. In 1993, green outdoor clothing pioneer Patagonia proudly introduced fleece sweaters made from plastic trash. That seemed a perfect solution from a progressive company. Today, we know that fleece is a major contributor to the rapid increase of the amount of plastic microparticles that pollute soil, rivers and oceans.

The microparticles are also the reason that cleaning up the oceans is an illusion. Plastic is everywhere in the seas. There are no places where the pollution concentrates. The *Great Pacific Garbage Patch* has become a popular term evoking the image of an island of waste that can be cleaned up. But such an island does not exist. The plastic waste sinks and breaks down under fierce winds and currents. The plastic pieces get smaller and smaller, but the molecules remain intact. Clean-up initiatives have generated a great deal of attention for the plastic soup problem. Dutch inventor Boyan Slat became world famous at age 16 when he came up with a collection system using ocean currents. His and other initiatives have substantially contributed to more public awareness, and even raised a lot of money for the fight against plastic pollution. That's a good thing. But it does not mean that it is possible to clean up the oceans with manmade technology like the robot that cleans up a swimming pool.

In 2002, some 150 coastal towns in 13 Northern European countries launched *Fishing for Litter*. When fish is sorted, the plastic that has also been caught is collected separately in bags that can contain up to 250 kilograms of waste. In the harbor, these bags are taken to recycling facilities. Fishing for Litter is a laudable initiative to do the right thing when confronted with waste. Yet, it is a meaningless effort given the fact that *every minute* a garbage truck load of plastic is dumped in the ocean. And we are not even talking about the fact that the collected waste more than likely cannot be effectively recycled because it contains an unclear mix of plastics with undisclosed toxic additives.

We have to stop the plastic pollution on land before the waste gets dumped in the oceans. That means we need to change distribution and consumption patterns. In 2014, in Berlin and Antwerp, the first packaging-free, zero-waste stores were opened. Customers buy, for instance, wooden toothbrushes. They put their eggs, sugar and pasta in containers they bring themselves and they pay by weight. In 2019, a major British supermarket chain, Waitrose, began similar experiments removing plastic from 200 product lines while encouraging their customers to bring in their own containers.

The US-based startup Loop works with multinationals like Nestlé, Procter & Gamble, PepsiCo, and Unilever to deliver tea, pasta and even juices in reusable packaging without any plastics. So far, Loop is testing its services only in selected markets. Loop's founder, Tom Szaky, says: "If our mission is to eliminate waste, then recycling is not the long-term solution. We need to completely rethink our relationship to products and how we shop". Splosh is another startup. The company sells concentrated household cleaners, laundry soap and body wash by mail. The goods come in small pouches and then need to be diluted at home. This way Splosh saves plastic and distribution costs. Colgate-Palmolive has spent five years developing a recyclable tube for its toothpastes. To make the tube easily recyclable, they had to get rid of the thin layer of aluminum inside. It will take until 2025 for Colgate to present all its toothpastes in this new tube. And then the consumer still faces the challenge of deciding in which bin to put the empty tube…

Increasingly, restaurants present themselves as "plastics free". Paper is an obvious candidate for alternative packaging. However, that old-fashioned "paper or plastic" debate has become complex too. In recent decades, the structures of many types of papers have been improved with plastic (!) layers to resist moisture and to be more competitive with plastics…

Plastic-Free July is an Australian initiative started in 2011. Today, there are more than two million people in 160 countries that refuse the use of plastic products in the month of July. The initiative provides consumers with advice how to avoid the use of plastics, such as which alternatives exist for plastic drinking straws for children or how you can make your own toothpaste and eliminate that polluting plastic tube.

Initiatives like Plastic-Free July highlight the fact that most plastic is only very briefly used. Plastic packaging represents about 40 percent of the global plastic production. We need to eliminate that packaging waste. One simple fact illustrates the scope of that challenge: from a climate change perspective, one ton of food waste has the impact of three tons of packaging waste. In other words: if preventing packaging food leads to more food waste, we are only adding to our problems.

In the meantime, the amount of plastic packaging is only rising as more and more things are packaged in smaller and smaller units. Calls to ban single use plastics become increasingly louder. In 2002, Bangladesh became the first country in the world to ban plastic bags after they were found to be clogging drainage systems amid the devastating floods that regularly hit the country. Since then more than 140 countries, including China, India, Georgia, Colombia, Rwanda, Zimbabwe and some 30 more African countries, have implemented taxes or partial bans on plastics. At the same time, in many of these countries, compliance is an obvious challenge.

South Korea is the first industrialized nation where in 2019 a law took effect banning most plastic bags. The Korean government issues steep fines if retailers fail to comply. The European Union will implement a ban on single-use plastics by 2021. Interestingly enough, the EU made an exception for paper covered with plastic film. Canada has recently announced the intention to execute the same ban and will probably allow the same exception. A success for the lobby of the paper industry, not for the environment.

Single-use bans seem to make sense. Using precious and polluting resources to only briefly package and ship goods, is wasteful. However, on a closer examination such bans do not provide a real long-term solution. They do not change production structures and methods. Single-use bans are mostly crisis management by politicians who want to show their voters that they are finally responding to their concerns. The point is that plastic bags are not necessarily bad. It depends on how they are designed and used. Here's an example: You buy fruits and vegetables in a store and take them home in a compostable plastic bag. After you have made your salad you put the peels and the waste in the biodegradable bag that is ready for composting and generating healthy humus for your plants. That single-use bag is no longer a "single-use" bag and should not be banned. To the contrary: that bag reduces the need to collect organic municipal waste and, at the same time, helps increasing composting and replenishing the soil.

Rather than banning plastics, we should ensure that the functional use is in line with the technical capability and embed their use in well-designed policies. We need to engineer and design the end of life of plastic products before we introduce them in the market.

From the very start, a catastrophic design failure lies at the core of the plastic pollution. In 1907, Belgian-American chemist Leo Baekeland developed "Bakelite", the first plastic made from synthetic components. Bakelite infiltrated virtually all aspects of our lives in the first half of the 20th century. It was used to make toys, for electrical and insulation products, even for jewelry. Because it was such an easy and adaptable product, nobody thought about the impact of the ingredients on people and society. Bakelite contains formaldehyde, asbestos and extremely toxic polymers. Today, bakelite is considered a "silent killer". It needed to be removed and, even decades after its prohibition, it is still brought to special facilities where it is being disposed of.

We know the health risks that bakelite poses. The reality is that we do not know most of the dangers that come with modern plastics. There is a lot of secrecy in the plastics industry about the use of additives that provide strategic advantages. Like the contribution of Mr. Baekeland over a hundred years ago, today's functionality prevails over any concerns about the long-term impact of innovations. Even when we know the problem, we do not act. The plastics industry fights any attempt to regulate the use of flame retardants creating an unsolvable dilemma for politicians: do you want to die in a fire or from cancer?

Such dilemmas do not need to exist if we start design and production with awareness and responsibility. There is an overwhelming need for intelligent design. Such design needs to incorporate how a plastic breaks down—degrades—in time. Already in the 1980s in Brazil, chemists were experimenting with creating polymers from sugar cane. Initially these attempts were driven by the fear that we would run out of oil. Imperial Chemical Industries (ICI) introduced Biopol as a first biodegradable plastic in the 1980s as well. The European Commission began defining "biodegradation" in policies in the early 1990s. By now, we have gone through four decades of research and policymaking but there is still a lot of confusion about degradation.

Many products proudly announce that their packaging material is "biodegradable". That means the material will degrade in soil under the influence of micro-organisms. However, if the same material ends up in water, it does not degrade for centuries. It will simply break down in ever smaller pieces. European farmland already has up to 400 kilograms of plastic waste per hectare. In the African Sahara (!) you will find on average some 40 kilograms of plastic per hectare. The material that is left in the desert, in a meadow or a forest only exposed to the sun and the weather, will remain intact for centuries. Biodegradable only means that a molecule is designed to be decomposed by bacteria in soil or in industrial composting facilities—but not for decomposition in sun or water, and certainly not in salt (a preservative!) sea water. There are still no standards for photo degradation of plastics in the sun or a different kind of decomposition in water. The same bacteria that break down plastic in soil simply do not live in water.

From time to time, scientific journals enthusiastically announce that a scientist has been able to manipulate an organism to breakdown plastic, for instance, in water or in soil. These are great innovations that often mimic what nature does. However, unless we are succeeding in designing plastics that will invariably degrade in a short time frame in all conditions, we won't be able to successfully tackle plastic pollution. There are companies that are succeeding in meeting that challenge and we will be addressing those initiatives in chapter 6. The critical observation must be that no scientific solution will work without a business model. The recycling and repurposing of plastics has to become economical and profitable. The transformation of the plastics industry depends on the redesign of the 100,000s of molecules for degradation in all three conditions: sun, sea and soil. That vast project is only going to succeed within a successful economic model.

For years, cosmetics companies have put microplastics in their products like moisturizing creams and sunscreens. Polymers were the second most important ingredient in these products after water. Today we find these microparticles everywhere in the oceans. The leaders of the cosmetics industry are keen to tell us that they are no longer using these synthetic polymers. However, they remain painfully silent when it comes to contributing meaningful solutions to cleaning up the mess—the collateral damage—they created over decades.

Industry leaders voice their support for bioplastics and single use bans at "the future of plastics" conferences. Conveniently nobody talks about the plastics lobby in the United States that is desperately fighting to keep profiting from the worst pollution in the world. Soft drink giants introduce plastic bottles that contain small percentages of biodegradable plastic.

They invite applause as they claim that given the number of plastic water bottles consumed, even that minor percentage has a meaningful impact on the plastic problem. At the Nestlé headquarters in Vevey, Switzerland, 50 scientists are working fulltime to develop new—non-plastic—packaging materials for brands such as KitKat, Perrier and Purina pet food. But the Swiss giant acknowledges that it does not see a future without plastics. Nestlé currently produces 1.7 million tons of plastic packaging a year. And nobody has any plan to stop the ongoing horrendous dumping of plastic in the oceans. That crisis is not part of "the future of plastics".

The innovation in the industry is still focused on improving functionality and performance through combinations and multiple layers of different plastics and metals. That creative energy needs to go designing and into developing a vision for the use of plastics in an integrated and regenerative economy.

Photo: © Copyright Julien Girardot R4W TAHITI-313.

Chapter 4

A boat with a message

In 2012, the catamaran "Planet Solar" became the first vessel to sail around the world using solar energy only. The journey of the world's biggest solar catamaran was focused on raising awareness about the potential for solar energy to reverse global warming. In 2015, after Planet Solar had completed its voyage, the German owner, Immo Ströher, offered the boat to the Race for Water Foundation. That seemed a generous gift, but—as any sailboat owner knows—owning a boat is expensive. It costs a lot of money to maintain a sailboat in good condition. It only makes sense if you sail a lot or you have special mission for the boat.

We decided that the mission of the Race for Water Foundation would be best served with a truly remarkable and innovative boat. We began the journey to turn a modern, state-of-the-art, sailing boat into a 100 percent ecological vessel that would show the world that we can clean up marine transportation. In our vision, only a vessel solely powered by clean and renewable energy could raise awareness about the plastic pollution in the oceans in a convincing and effective way.

The Race for Water catamaran looks like a futuristic floating spaceship covered with 512 square meters of solar panels. The solar panels power batteries that feed an electric engine. The boat has no mast. Nevertheless, it can sail. It uses a large 40 square meters towing kite with a shape similar to a paraglider that propels the boat forward. The kite operates at an altitude of between 100 and 150 meters where winds are stronger and more stable. The kite can only be used, when the boat sails downwind. In other wind conditions, the boat uses propellers driven by the electric engine.

Race for Water uses a version of a major German innovation that combines the ancient kite technology with two other antique inventions: the yoyo and the cuckoo clock. The wind energy system was developed by SkySails, a company based in Hamburg. Using the yoyo system, a kite is pulled intermittently using artificial intelligence and a robot to most efficiently benefit from the conditions. This mechanical force is subsequently transformed into the modulated power of a cuckoo clock. This modulation is critical to make sure that the turbine that generates electricity is fed evenly despite wildly volatile wind conditions at up to 800 meters high. For instance: Typical wind turbines, that don't even reach these high altitudes where the wind always blows, are automatically turned off in stormy conditions to prevent the propeller from spinning out of control. The combined technologies of the yoyo and the cuckoo clock enable the consistent use of a kite to harvest wind energy on land in all conditions. Artificial intelligence is also used to make sure that the kite stays in the permitted range and does not interfere with surrounding

Photo: © Copyright Julien Girardot R4W TAHITI-247.

Photo: © Copyright Julien Girardot R4W TAHITI-88.

objects. Furthemore, the robot of the kite responds to the transponders of aircraft and automatically adjusts the kite to stay out of the range of the approaching plane. The Race for Water version of the SkySails kite has a range of 150 meters and only uses the cuckoo clock technology to pull a boat at sea.

During the night the engine can be operated on battery power. The batteries can also power the boat during overcast days when the solar panels do not charge well. However, batteries do run empty. A sailboat always faces a tradeoff between adding more batteries—and more weight—and the risk that the boat runs out of power and needs to wait for the sun to come back to power up the systems. That's why sail boats have backup engines powered by diesel. And diesel is a dirty fossil fuel…

Race for Water had to find a different solution. The boat sails around the world to host events on carefully selected dates involving conferences, meetings with government leaders et cetera. In other words: The Race for Water Odyssey has an agenda that needs to be followed. The initiative needed more power on the boat to make sure that a few overcast days would not derail its mission. That need led to a major innovation.

Like most ships that sail the oceans, the boat has a desalination machine to produce fresh water. The Race for Water boat, however, also has two elektrolyzers that produce hydrogen on board. Hydrogen is a very efficient energy vector. It can keep energy stored for a long time. The boat can store 200 kilogram of hydrogen in 25 pressurized bottles. When necessary, two fuel cells can convert the hydrogen into electricity.

The elektrolyzers produce hydrogen with surplus solar energy only when the boat is docked or towed by the kite. The energy needed for the electrolysis should not compete with the electricity that the propellers need to power the boat at sea. The hydrogen system adds six days of autonomy to the Race for Water boat. Today, the boat can continue its journey without sun or wind for a total of eight days. The chance that there is no sun on the oceans for more than eight days is miniscule. After sailing 30,000 miles across the Atlantic, and South Pacific oceans, the statistics show that the hydrogen backup is rarely used: 67 percent of the energy that the boat uses comes from the solar panels; 24 percent from the kite, and only 9 percent from the stored hydrogen.

Using saltwater and the sun to produce electricity—and drinking water—is a technology that has been around for a long time. The fuel cell was invented in 1838. Nonetheless, the Race for Water boat became the first vessel powered by hydrogen only a few years ago. The technology adds a major element to the Race for Water mission. The boat sails to many islands and coastal communities that are heavily impacted by plastic pollution. These are mostly poor communities where electricity is often provided by generators that run on polluting, expensive, and imported diesel. Race for Water demonstrates to these communities that today's hydrogen technology is mature, reliable and sustainable and provides a clean alternative to fossil fuel-based energy production. The message is powerful: wherever there is sun, seawater and wind, you can have power, and water for drinking and agriculture, and you can change the future of a community. One 40 square meter kite can generate enough energy for 2,500 families! The Maldives are the first country in the world that is ready to adopt the kites as energy source. These islands in the Indian Ocean do not have enough space for extensive arrays of solar panels and their ground structure is not solid enough to support conventional wind turbines.

The decision to present the mission of Race for Water through the journey of the biggest solar catamaran in the world has paid off. We know we have a good and important message. But we also know that nobody likes talking about waste. It is a depressing topic. However, it is very different to invite people for a visit to a unique sustainable boat for a difficult conversation about pollution and preserving the oceans. Everybody—from local environmental activists to businesspeople and government leaders—wants to come and experience our boat. The innovative boat has also helped Race for Water to attract high profile support for its mission. Swiss luxury watchmaker Breguet owned by the Hayek family has become the lead sponsor of the initiative.

All the influencers and thought leaders who visit the boat have the same experience. They come to see inspiring innovation and, once they are on board, they hear our story about the terrible plastic problem, and about the sustainable solutions we can implement. Our boat has been built to host events. We can have conferences, workshops and classes with more than 80 participants. The boat usually spends one or two months at each stopover and during these weeks every day five classes of schoolchildren visit. The children learn about clean energy and plastic pollution. After their visits, the children continue their experience with special educational tools that have been developed by Race for Water.

With the visiting school classes, workshops and conferences we serve two of the three pillars of the mission of Race for Water: *learn* and *share*. The learning part of the mission is also served by visiting teams of scientists from universities around the world. The scientists join the ocean crossings to take samples of marine life and water, and to observe plastic pollution around islands and coastal areas. Initial research is done in the especially designed 90 square meters onboard lab before the findings are sent to the universities for further analysis and study.

In 2015, the first Race for Water odyssey was a 10-month journey across seven oceans with a regular sailing trimaran. During this expedition scientists of the University of Bordeaux confirmed that the majority of the plastic pollution is not concentrated in large "gyres" but rather has broken down in microplastics that pollute marine life everywhere. The team collected samples from 30 beaches along the Atlantic Pacific and Indian oceans. While the scientists are still studying the data and the eco-toxicological effects of microplastics on cells, embryos and larvae of fish, the expedition already made abundantly clear that plastic pollution needs to be stopped on land—before it reaches the oceans!

In 2017, a second Race of Water "odyssey of hope" with the new solar catamaran began in France under the motto "plastic waste is the problem *and* the solution". This five-year expedition is scheduled to coincide with major international events like the World Expo in Dubai in 2021. The expedition

SUN, WIND AND WATER
Sole sources of energy for the *Race for Water* vessel

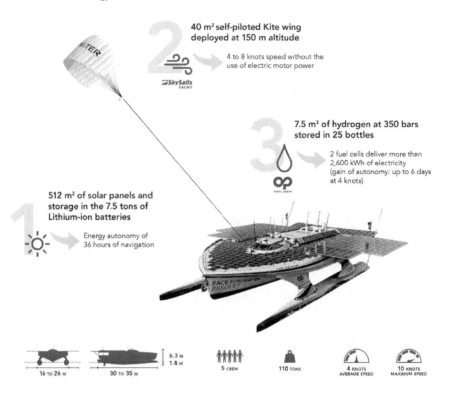

40 m² self-piloted Kite wing deployed at 150 m altitude

4 to 8 knots speed without the use of electric motor power

SkySails
YACHT

7.5 m³ of hydrogen at 350 bars stored in 25 bottles

2 fuel cells deliver more than 2,600 kWh of electricity (gain of autonomy: up to 6 days at 4 knots)

512 m² of solar panels and storage in the 7.5 tons of Lithium-ion batteries

Energy autonomy of 36 hours of navigation

16 TO 26 M

30 TO 35 M

6.3 M
1.8 M

5 CREW

110 TONS

4 KNOTS
AVERAGE SPEED

10 KNOTS
MAXIMUM SPEED

Caption: Livre schema energies bateau eng

will visit 38 cities and communities during the five years. During these stopovers, the boat is expected to host 50,000 children, and business and government leaders. The five-year expedition will also host some ten scientific research missions.

Already, biologists from Chile have been conducting a study about the impact of plastic pollution on seabirds around Easter Island. Scientists from Germany, Norway and Cuba have been on board to study the microplastic pollution of the oceans. Researchers from the Netherlands came for a "plastisphere" project. This term refers to new ecosystems that develop under the influence of plastic pollution. Scientists from Fiji have been evaluating the microplastics in the surface waters between Tonga and Fiji. Scientists from France and Belgium have been doing the same sampling in the waters around Guadeloupe in the Caribbean and the microplastics impacts have been studied on coral reef in New Caledonia.

All these scientific expeditions benefit from the fact that the Race for Water boat sails at low speeds which makes it easy to take samples and measurements from the afterdeck with direct access to the sea. The scientific research is also supported by the fact that there is no noise or fuel pollution.

A final part of Race for Water's learning mission relates to the research of plastic pollution on land. Everywhere the boat docks, Race for Water staff spend time analyzing the pollution and waste infrastructure in the community. The staff write extensive reports about each community and collect data that are critical to the solution to stop the plastic pollution that Race for Water is going to implement.

With its expeditions around the world, Race for Water

demonstrates the existence of practical solutions for preserving the oceans as well as the clean future of marine transportation. The last pillar of the Race for Water mission is *act*. We serve that part of our mission with our solution to stop the plastic pollution of the oceans. We can stop 80 percent of that pollution in the next decade while generating jobs and clean energy. In chapter 8 we will explain how we are going to do that.

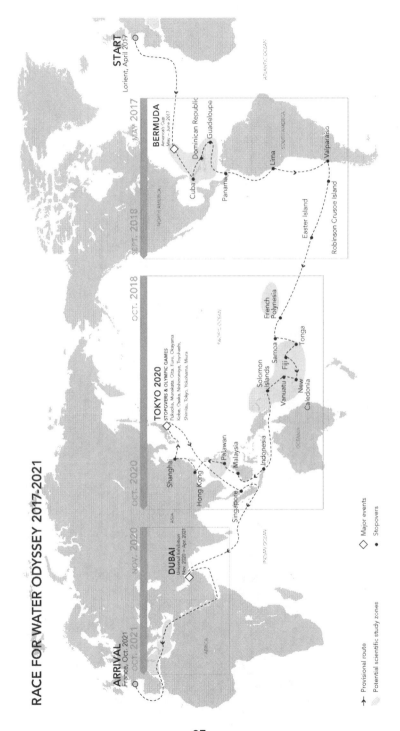

RACE FOR WATER ODYSSEY 2017-2021

START
Lorient, April 2017

BERMUDA
America's Cup
May – June 2017

Cuba
Dominican Republic
Guadeloupe
Panama
Lima
Valparaíso
Easter Island
Robinson Crusoe Island

French Polynesia
Samoa
Tonga
Solomon Islands
Fiji
Vanuatu
New Caledonia

TOKYO 2020
STOPOVERS & OLYMPIC GAMES
Fukuoka, Munakata, Oita, Kure, Okayama
Kobe, Osaka, Nishinomiya, Toyohashi,
Shimizu, Tokyo, Yokohama, Miura

Shanghai
Hong Kong
Palawan
Malaysia
Indonesia
Singapore

DUBAI
Universal Exhibition
Nov. 2020 – Apr. 2021

ARRIVAL
France, Oct. 2021

MAY 2017
SEPT. 2018
OCT. 2018
OCT. 2020
NOV. 2020
OCT. 2021

ATLANTIC OCEAN
NORTH AMERICA
SOUTH AMERICA
PACIFIC OCEAN
OCEANIA
ASIA
AFRICA
INDIAN OCEAN

↑ Provisional route
◇ Major events
• Stopovers
Potential scientific study zones

The Plastic Solutions

Chapter 5
Objectives and principles: Plastic and soil

Today, we live in a wonderful world full of choice and variety. Supermarkets offer many variations of the same things in different structures and different kinds of packaging—from toothbrushes to soaps and from milk to eggs, and even a slice of meat or a single cookie is individually packaged. Going online quickly multiplies the amount of available choices and options, and the wrapping only increases. In communities where people live comparable lives, very few people use the exact same things (brands) on a daily basis. That's the reality of modern life under the influence of marketing and globalization.

The same reality poses an enormous challenge for regulation and policy making. It is a daunting task to capture all options and possibilities in clear and usable legislation. Laws become thick books full of categories and exceptions. Far too often, even the politicians who pass the laws have no complete understanding of the rules they lay down, and hardly ever outdated rules are eliminated. Rightly, entrepreneurs and business managers have long complained about bureaucracy that stands in the way of economic development and innovation. In response, politicians have made deregulation a rallying call in elections around the world.

It is impossible to write rules that cover all situations in a highly complex world. That same reality applies to the plastics industry too. There is a big difference between the plastic bag that contains the peels and leftovers of the lunch salad and that is used for a few days, and the underground PVC pipe that distributes water to homes in the neighborhood that should last for half a century. The plastic bag should degrade quickly and turn into healthy soil with the composting peels bringing back the nutrients to the land. That bag is an important instrument for much necessary generation of soil. At the same time, we do not want the PVC pipe to degrade quickly. That would be the end of our water supply. Nevertheless, we also do not want that PVC pipe over hundreds of years, when water systems have been replaced and changed, to break down in plastic microparticles that will pollute the lives of future generations.

Any good policy has to start with an understanding of waste. In fact, with the understanding that waste does not exist. Nature does not produce waste. In nature, any substance is always a resource for a new process in never-ending loops of regeneration. A tree drops its leaves which are converted through armies of species including earthworms, ants, fungi, micro-organisms into humus— soil—which blended with rain and bird poop feeds the tree again through the roots. The same soil that feeds the trees, maintains all life—including ours.

The tree is at the center of a web of life and stands amidst a network of mushrooms that looks like a neural system. The example clearly shows the complex relationship between waste and soil and that linear, segmented approaches that dominate all industries can never succeed in getting rid of pollution. The point is that failing waste policies go hand in hand with soil degradation. There is a need for a quantum leap in policy making. Policies should not just be focused on protection of the environment; they should be focused on the regeneration of nature.

The European Union under the leadership of the progressive Italian Commissioner for the Environment, Carlo Ripa di Meana, was the first in the world to introduce a standard for biodegradation for packaging and packaging waste in 1994. "Biodegradable packaging waste shall be of such a nature that it is capable of undergoing physical, chemical, thermal or biological decomposition such that most of the finished compost ultimately decomposes into carbon dioxide, biomass and water", reads Directive 94/62. It does NOT say that the package should decompose in the three main depositories on the planet: soil, sun and water.

In 2018, almost 25 years later, the EU took another step with a ban on the single use of the top 10 plastics found on European beaches as well as fishing gear. Directive 2019/904 bans the items that cause most of the ocean pollution like plastic cotton bud sticks, cutlery, plastic shopping bags, plates, straws, drink stirrers and sticks for balloons by

2021. The new EU directive highlights the challenge for regulation. Under the new rules a compostable bag used to take compostable food leftovers to a compost heap in a garden is banned. That does not make sense.

The problem is that we do not have a vision of how to integrate waste in the economy and make sure that soil is continuously regenerated. That's why the pollution of the environment and the degradation of soil will continue as long as we stick to the same business model and policy framework. We haven't formulated policies for the reuse of sewage. Banning certain plastics is something else than envisioning the end use of a product as a resource for something else.

There is a clear starting point. When it comes to environmental regulation, the EU is considered the global pioneer. In article 191 of Treaty on the Functioning of the European Union, it is stated that all policies should "be based on the *precautionary principle* and on the principles that preventive action should be taken, that environmental damage should as a priority be rectified at the source and that the polluter should pay".

Principle 1: The precautionary principle

The precautionary principle should be the overriding principle when it comes to all matters relating to public health and the environment. However, we will only be able to stop the accumulation of plastic waste when we add "according to functionality"—"shelf life"—to this principle. The same rules for composting and biodegradation cannot apply to car tires, water pipes, tooth brushed and plastic bags.

Principle 2: All is renewable

A second essential principle relates to the source of plastics. Obviously, all plastic should be created from non-fossil fuel, renewable resources. Nature is a remarkable producer of all kinds of polymers, each tailored to the needs of that particular species. However, the manufacturing of plastics can never be allowed to compete with food. In the past we have seen that the manipulation of corn for the industrial processes including plastics drove up the price of tortillas in poor communities in developing countries. Such corn-based plastics may be biodegradable, but their production at the expense of food for poor people is clearly unacceptable, and unnecessary as there are plenty of other options to create sustainable polymers. It sounds like the palm oil story in chapter 2: biodegradable but certainly not sustainable. There are better options. For instance, polymers can be made from hemp, silk, thistles and seaweed and the cultivation of these resources comes with many additional benefits—sequestering carbon, recycling minerals—without competing with food resources.

From the choice of the source for the manufacturing of the plastics follows the ultimate objective: all plastic at the end of its functional life should degrade in soil, sun and water. But not just *degrade* without causing harm; the degradation should ultimately *replenish* the soil like the falling leaves of the tree. From ashes to ashes, it is said about human life. This is the guiding principle: everything comes from the soil and everything should go back to it. Any other strategy eventually leads to the collapse of the nutrient cycles.

Principle 3: Extended producer responsibility

A third principle relates to the role of the manufacturer. Companies need to be responsible for the impact of their products on the environment and on society. That responsibility should not simply end the moment the sale is concluded and/or the product warranty has expired. Policymakers talk about "extended producer responsibility" (EPR). Manufacturers are deemed responsible for the entire lifecycle of their products including the waste—or better: "next life"—phase. EPR is already quite well adopted in industries like car tires and batteries, where usable raw materials can easily be reclaimed. With plastics we are still far away from that. The industry is hiding behind excuses: The plastic producer of a thin film that covers a paper cup is not held responsible when the polymer does not degrade in the sun because the cup has an ultraviolet blocking agent that the paper manufacturer added to the cup. Et cetera.

Principle 4: What is put together, can be taken apart

Production processes have to be changed to allow for the recovery of raw materials. That includes ending the practice of manufacturing multi-layered plastics to allow for specific performances. Today, it is common for engineers to design products that are produced at high speed from complex combinations of plastics, paper and thin aluminum foil that nobody can take apart. The simple rule has to be that nothing can be produced that nobody knows how to take apart. The lazy fix of the landfill is slowly losing ground. However, today's preferred fix—incineration—leads to a total loss of useful elements and the exhaust of toxic gases.

When it comes to the responsibility of the industry, we still need even more. Not only do we need diaper companies and other manufacturers of complex plastics to stop their polluting production. We also need them to be responsible for the mess they have created in the past decades. For years, the cosmetics industry added plastic micro particles to products like hydrating gels and sunscreens. While the big brands swear that they have abandoned that practice, the micro particles from the past are now everywhere in the oceans. As we will see in the coming chapters, it will cost a lot of money to clean up that pollution. The companies that caused the disaster should be first in line to take responsibility for the cleanup. That's true *extended* producer responsibility. Stopping making a mess is simply not good enough.

The combination of the precautionary principle based on functionality, the renewable principle based on resources that are not competing with food production, the principle of extended producer responsibility, and finally the principle that whatever is put together can be taken apart again, lays the foundation for regulation that will start to reverse the devastating trend of worldwide plastic pollution and could turn the production of plastics into an activity that ultimately regenerates the soil as the foundation of life. We do not have to envision a new bureaucratic nightmare of regulation. In fact, when clearly formulated, these guiding principles do not allow for grey zones, vagueness, lobbyists and other ardent defenders of a logic of the past. They make the responsibilities for the production and use of plastics very clear. So, now that we know how to introduce healthy and sustainable production, let's clean up the mess.

Chapter 6

Wasting or using waste?

The United Nations established the Intergovernmental Panel on Climate Change (IPCC) in 1988 as a response to the—at the time—emerging crisis of global warming. Over the years, the IPCC has extensively reported on climate change patterns and related energy forecasts. It took the panel more than 30 years to publish the first report solely dedicated to "Climate Change and Land" in 2019. The report warns that global warming is increasing droughts, soil erosion, and wildfires while expanding deserts and diminishing crop yields in many parts of the world. The report adds grim notes to the observation of the UN's Food and Agricultural Organization (FAO) that intensive agriculture has already degraded one third of the soil on the planet through salinization, chemical pollution and depletion of nutrients. It is an unfolding disaster in which the plastic crisis plays a major role. At the same time, plastic can be part of the solution.

Humans exploit 72 percent of the ice-free surface of the planet to feed, clothe and support themselves. Without fertile soil, there is no life. And, one of the most glaring conclusions of the IPCC report is that soil is being lost more than 100 times faster than it is being formed in agricultural areas where farmers use ploughs—which applies to most agriculture. Soil is being lost 10 to 20 times faster even on fields that are not tilled. Farming is at a collision course with nature that needs some 2,000 years to create 10 centimeters of soil. In the meantime, the way we spoil soil contributes a lot to global warming. Plants and forests can absorb the warming CO_2 gas from the air and fix it in soil. However, instead of the land being a sink for CO_2, modern agriculture and land use are responsible for about a quarter of greenhouse emissions.

We are not only losing vital soil, the soil that we have is no longer as rich as it used to be. As a result, the food we eat is not as nutritious as the food of our grandparents. Research shows that, in the past 50 years, potatoes have lost half of their copper and iron, a third of their calcium, half of their vitamin C, and almost all their vitamin A. Broccoli—often recommended as a cancer-busting superfood—today has 80 percent less copper than in 1940. You would have to eat 10 tomatoes today to get the same amount of copper as from one tomato 80 years ago, and you need to eat eight oranges to get the same amount of vitamin A as your grandparents from one orange. We continue to price food by weight whereas the real value comes from the nutritional content that depends on the quality of the soil.

These are just some stark examples. Studies show the same pattern of nutrients depletion across dozens of other fruits and vegetables. We think that eating a fruit or a vegetable offers a constant value for our health. That is not the case. Nutritional value is directly linked to the quality of the soil.

A plant can't provide nutrients to a human that it can't take from the soil. The food that intensive agriculture provides, increasingly resembles dust with added chemical fertilizer. Yes, organic produce offers more nutrients, but it does not escape the overall trend of nutrients depletion.

More than 500 years ago, Leonardo da Vinci foresaw the crisis we are in today. He warned that wrongful waste management—discarding precious resources—would undermine the future of food production *and* humanity. We are not only wasting soil; we are also wasting waste. Da Vinci realized that human health would benefit from sanitation through sewage collection. But he also knew that human waste contained valuable nutrients that should not be carelessly discarded. Today, sewage sludge may be treated, it is hardly ever *used* in a productive way. And other waste is sent to unproductive landfills.

There is no other species that uses diapers to take vital resources out of the cycles of life and puts them into landfills and sewage pipes. The disposable diaper was invented in Sweden in 1942. The innovation was supported by a visionary government to promote gender equality and to reduce the household burden on working mothers. It was a great social invention. It also was the beginning of a huge, very profitable and very polluting industry. Millions of genetically modified pine trees are continuously harvested in the tropics to supply the fluff that is to absorb the excrement. Petroleum is used to create triple layers of different plastics and a magical acrylic is added to absorb 500 times more liquid than a baby can ever release just to make certain that babies will feel dry and never dread the artificial layer around their bodies. Babies used to discard diapers—cloth or plastic—the moment they began to crawl and walk since the wetness made them feel cold. By adding the super absorbers, infants feel no discomfort and diaper use prolongs from 9-10 months to 3-4 years. A financial bonanza, a serious health risk, and a massive explosion of waste.

An average baby uses six to eight diapers every day or between 6,500 and 10,000 diapers before toilet training is complete. That leads to staggering numbers. Babies in the United States, the world leader in diaper consumption, use an estimated 25 billion disposable diapers each year producing some 3.5 million tons of waste. That's enough to fill a major football stadium some 15 times. Diapers are big moneymakers for multinationals like Procter & Gamble (Pampers) and Kimberly-Clark (Huggies) that aggressively market them as symbols of modernity. They have even convinced nonprofits in the United States to support low-income family's ability to buy diapers. Each year, the US celebrates "diaper need awareness week". The annual expense for diapers comes to $1,000 and can be prohibitive for a family living on the minimum wage of $15,000 a year. Studies show that poor people skip buying basic necessities (food) to be able to buy diapers. At the same time, these corporations are eagerly eyeing the fast-emerging middle class in populous countries like China, India and Indonesia to vastly expand their markets.

Furthermore, the diaper corporations continue investing in clever innovative strategies to generate more sales. Recently,

Procter & Gamble (P&G) made frontpage news announcing that it was introducing *smart nappies*. These diapers use sensors, software and video to monitor when babies sleep, wee and poo. That incomprehensible innovation stands in sharp contrast with the almost complete failure of the recycling of diapers. In Italy, P&G has established a joint venture that has built a plant capable of recycling 8,000 tons of disposable diapers into plastic bottle caps, viscose clothing, school desks and urban playgrounds each year. In New Zealand, Kimberly-Clark is composting nappies into soil for landscaping while discarding the plastics which cannot be recovered.

These window-dressing initiatives do not change the fact that the diaper industry causes gigantic pollution. It takes about 200 milliliters (a glass) of crude oil to produce the plastic ingredients for one diaper. That means that worldwide millions of barrels of oil are used every year to produce something that's being used for a few hours. It is arguably the most senseless use of oil. Subsequently, the complex plastic compositions stay intact in landfills for hundreds of years while the accumulation of human waste becomes a breeding ground for disease. In developing countries nappies often end up in other places, including in rice paddies, rivers and oceans, where they contribute to the plastic pollution problem.

Moreover, diapers contain all kinds of secretive substances that make them absorb better but that are not necessarily healthier for babies or for the planet. Childhood asthma has been linked to inhaling the mixtures of chemicals emitted from diapers. Some diapers still contain phthalates, the plastic softeners that have been banned from toys. All these toxins keep leaking into the environment. The same toxins raise questions about the recycling efforts. Do we want children to play at playgrounds or to sit at school desks made from recycled diapers without any manufacturer disclosing which additives were used in the design to outperform the competition? Children should never be exposed to chemicals that we do not know.

The point is that failing waste policies go hand-in-hand with soil degradation. As Leonardo da Vinci knew, when we harvest plants for food, we take vital nutrients from the soil. When we subsequently do not give these nutrients back, the soil gets depleted. Composting biomass boosts the activity of microbes and fungi in the soil and these organisms help release the nutrients into plants. Similarly, human waste is filled with nutrients from the food we eat. These nutrients were taken from the soil and they are essential for restoring the soil. Breast milk has an extraordinary nutritional value as it has to kickstart new life. Baby's poo, therefor, contains unique micro-organisms that should never be wasted.

The solution to the problem of soil degradation begins with re-orienting the flow of high-quality waste and re-establishing a fundamental cycle of life. The good news is that it is already being done. For example: A few years ago, in Berlin, an initiative was launched to offer young parents free (!) compostable diapers made from bamboo, hemp and charcoal. In return for this gift with a value of at least € 50 per month, the parents have to weekly return a bag with the used diapers. The company, Dycle, uses a simple, small factory to turn the waste with biomass and charcoal (biochar) into *terra preta*, nutrients-rich black soil. The terra preta technique has been used for thousands of years to produce very rich soil. Soil analysis shows, for instance, that the Vikings and the Incas followed this traditional method. It helps explain the extreme fertility of their otherwise infertile soil that allowed them to wage wars and expand their empires.

The city of Berlin allows Dycle to add the soil to parks for the planting of fruit trees. The system is partly funded by the city purchasing the fruit trees. After some five years, each tree provides a minimum of 50 kilograms of fruit per year which can be eaten or turned into juice, jams and baby food. Berlin follows an historic example. In the 18th and 19th centuries, Prussian emperors were known to plant extensive fruit tree gardens around their Sanssouci Palace in nearby Potsdam. Planting fruit belts around cities with fruit trees grown in human waste closes a vital nutrients loop. The environment wins—new soil is generated, and more CO_2 is captured while bees and birds can thrive; citizens win—they can enjoy fruit tree blossoms in parks and gardens and pick free fruits; and the city wins—the cost of the fruit trees is less than the savings on trash collection and waste management.

Dycle provides a response to the diaper and plastic pollution as well as to the soil degradation. Dycle does not use fossil fuels-based plastics. Plastic can very well be part of this solution too. Dycle's compostable diapers can possibly be made even more user-friendly with plastics. And that does not have to change their biodegradability. Plastics are made from long, complex chains of molecules—polymers. Their biodegradability depends on how these polymers are created. The basic ingredients are oil and cellulose. Today, for the oil, we use mostly polluting fossil fuels. However, plastics can also be made with oils from plants. In fact, the oil we pump up from deep layers of the Earth was once created from plants too.

The reality is that there is an abundance of opportunities around us to create polymers that fit into natural cycles. If we would only *look* around us. The problem is that we have a very distorted view of nature. Modern agriculture only sees the crop that has been planted on the field. If something else starts to grow on the same field, it is called a "weed" and we use chemicals to destroy it. Who has decided that some parts of nature are weeds that cannot be used? There is a weird arrogance in that perspective as the following story illustrates.

Around the Mediterranean's millions of hectares of farmland have been left idle. These agricultural lands do not fit into the standardization practices that are supported by the agricultural policies of the European Union. The farmers may not use these fields, but that does not prevent nature from deciding what grows best in these places. It turns out to be that nature's "crop" for these lands is a thistle: Cardoon. Cardoon is from the artichoke family and the plant can grow up to three meters high. The thistle is growing wildly on an estimated 20 million hectares around the Mediterranean. Farmers have been attacking cardoon with herbicides for decades. Recently they have mostly used glyphosate, a broad-spectrum herbicide that the World Health Organization (WHO) has classified as "probably carcinogenic in humans".

But cardoon is a perennial plant and it keeps coming back. The reason is simple: The cardoon belongs there; it makes the best use of the space; it is nature's preferred plant to convert depleted soil back to fertile land.

The message from nature is that there is value in everything. And, as Italian scientists discovered, in cardoon, too. Novamont is an Italian company committed to an ecological economy and to finding sustainable sources for green chemistry. Novamont is a leading pioneer of biodegradable plastics. The company got involved in attempts to redevelop the economy of the island of Sardinia after the demise of the petrochemical industry based on cheap oil from Libya created a major economic downturn. Novamont's CEO, Dr. Catia Bastioli, led a team of scientists to study cardoon, that was growing everywhere on the island, in a pursuit to find value in the plant.

The scientists analyzed the biochemical composition of the flower, the seed, the stem and the roots, and discovered that cardoon has many uses. The plant has a flower that contains oil. The oil can be converted to an acid that can provide the main building block for a whole range of uses from mulching film for farming, to capsules for coffee machines, elastomers for medical gloves, and even for a pesticide. Note: The plant that refuses to be killed by glyphosate provides the raw materials for an herbicide that can be used to protect other crops in a healthy and sustainable way—*without* glyphosate. The oil can also be converted into a polymer that can be used to create the base ingredients for natural plastics. Finally, the same oil can be used as a lubricant for agricultural

equipment—replacing synthetic lubricants that pollute
the soil when they leak. Do you realize that the millions of
tractors, pickers, harvesters, cutters, shredders, sprayers, tillage
machines, and seeding, hay and forage equipment all use
synthetic smearing oils and greases that pollute the farms that
feed the world? A drop of that lubricant creates an infertility
spot in the soil for decades to come.

The "discovery" of cardoon offers insights into a world of
opportunities that remained hidden as the "weed" did not
fit in any productivity or profit strategy. The cardoon flower
has a white stuff on it that contains enzymatic bacteria that
have been used, for centuries, as the medium to make goat
cheese. The stem of cardoon is made up of cellulose, and that
contains sugars that can be turned into alcohol. The alcohol
and the acid can be used to create esters that are necessary
for creating polymers. The roots are rich ingredients that
are extraordinary for treating forehead wrinkles. And the
biomass, that is left after all the other processes, can be turned
into animal feed, or an excellent source of energy. All this
comes from a perennial plant that does not require planting,
fertilizing, or irrigation and does not need to be protected
with any herbicide or pesticide, a plant we call a weed.

Today, Novamont processes cardoon on Sardinia. Because
the plant can serve so many purposes, the farmer and
Novamont can adjust to market circumstances. If the market
demands more plastic, the harvest and production can
be directed in that direction. If the market requires more
herbicides, that is where the harvest and production will go.
Cardoon-based plastics can replace the elastomers for the

one-time use latex gloves in hospitals and food processing centers, or they can add a watertight layer to disposable and compostable diapers, or cardoon polymers can replace the plastic in hydrating gels. Cardoon allows the farmer and the industry to optimize the best for the land, for himself, for the consumer and for the planet.

Cardoon has also supported Novamont to become the world leader in bioplastics. The plant is one of the providers of the ingredients of the Mater-Bi family of biodegradable and compostable bioplastics that Novamont has developed over twenty-five years of research and innovation. The unique contribution of the company is that the Mater-Bi plastics degrade in sun, soil and water. There are bioplastics that degrade in soil; others that degrade in water. However, it is very rare for a bioplastic to degrade in all circumstances. The Novamont plastics will never create centuries of pollution anymore. At the same time, the properties of the bioplastics of Novamont are very similar to those of traditional plastics. They can replace almost every plastic application that is currently provided by the polluting fossil fuel-based plastics industry.

The combination of the Novamont and Dycle innovations shows that parents around the world can have the same very user-friendly diapers that they have gotten used to since the Swedes introduced them without causing any further pollution. Not only that, the used diapers and their very valuable contents, can be part of the much-needed restoration and replenishing of the soil that the IPCC argues for. Instead of solely focusing on regenerative farming techniques that only involve the farmers of the world, all new parents of the world become part of the soil restoration movement. If we redirect the flow of human waste back to the soil, and we add seaweed farming (see Chapter 8), we can massively regenerate soil and capture carbon emissions.

Of course, much more can and should be done. Today, the countries of the European Union, for instance, produce almost 100 million tons of organic waste that is mostly landfilled and burned—a huge waste causing greenhouse emissions. Disposable diapers are only a part of that waste. But that part may very well be enough to achieve the objective of the "4 per 1000" initiative. This French initiative suggests that an annual growth rate of 0.4 percent in the soil carbon stocks, or 4 permille per year, in the first 30-40 cm of soil, would be sufficient to compensate for the increase in CO_2 concentration in the atmosphere linked to human activities while at the same time improving soil fertility. As we wrote above, if left to nature alone, it takes 2,000 years to generate 10 centimeters of fertile soil. But, by using waste we already have, we can help nature and radically speed up the process.

The interesting fact is that plastic—that is, natural bioplastic—will be a major contributor to this effort. Bioplastics, bamboo, hemp and charcoal will transform the disposable diaper into a convenient, natural and healthy part of every baby's life. Incidentally, these new diapers will also save the trees that are now cut for the absorbing cellulose in pampers and huggies. That means a further contribution to reversing global warming as these trees can now continue to capture carbon emissions. It is clear in which direction diaper innovation of multinational corporations should go. The right plastic diapers provide a great opportunity to stop pollution and regenerate nature.

Chapter 7

Preventing fire, chemical cocktails and a healthy alternative

Plastics burn effortlessly. That shouldn't surprise us. They are made of the same fossil fuels that we burn to generate energy. But we do not want our television sets, the cushions of our sofas, our airline seats, our curtains, the mattresses of our beds, or the toys of our children to easily catch fire. That is why many of the products that we use every day are drenched in cocktails of chemicals called "flame-retardants".

The problem is that, in our understandable effort to prevent fire, we have created an enormous amount of toxicity in our environment. Plastics also contain other added chemicals to soften them or to block UV light to extend their life cycle. The plastics industry uses halogens, like fluorine, chlorine and bromine, phosphate esters, and ammonium, boron and sulphur compounds, and also heavy metals like mercury, tin, lead, and even arsenic. Many of these additives have been recognized as trade secrets. These compounds usually make up less than one percent of the volume and do not need to be disclosed. Of course, the industry argues that the quantities used are miniscule, safe, and tested through time. But it basically means that we are consuming chemical cocktails without any knowledge or understanding of the health risks.

The problem is that most of these additives are inert. That means they do not chemically bond with the plastics. Plastics release gases and decompose. As that happens, these chemicals easily migrate into the environment—the air we breathe, the dust on the floor, the water we drink—where they accumulate. The toxic chemicals are also part of the very plastic microparticles that are being found in every corner of the environment.

Toxic flame-retardants can be found in human breast milk and in fish. Research shows that the quantities are dramatically increasing, because these chemicals are not designed not to degrade. According to some reports the concentrations of the toxins are doubling every two to five years. Bromine compounds in blood and tissue of children are being associated with permanent brain damage and movement dysfunctions. High concentrations of arsenide in human spinal fluids are suspected to cause motor neuron diseases like Lou Gehrig's disease or amyotrophic lateral sclerosis (ALS). The number of people suffering from motor neuron diseases seems to increase annually.

Then there is the danger of chemicals that our bodies mistake as hormones. The structure of the pentabromo-di-phenyl ether molecule resembles the structure of the thyroid hormone thyroxine. When pentabromo-di-phenyl ether was forbidden some years ago, clever chemists replaced penta (5) with deca (10) to create decabromo-di-phenyl ether. However, when that molecule decomposes, it releases a similar toxic bromine gas.

It does not help that health regulations are set by parliaments that have very few members with a scientific background in chemistry. The representatives of the people are easy targets for lobby groups of industries that have a lot at stake. The annual value of the global flame-retardants market alone is $7 billion and grows with seven percent per year. These vast interests lead to absurd outcomes. Azodicarbonamide is a chemical that is strictly banned for the production of plastics. However, the same chemical—in "safe" concentrations—may be used in flour… And so, the toxins keep accumulating increasing health risks every day.

It is not for lack of an alternative. Nature has been containing fire for millennia. In nature, the exchange between heat and energy is managed through the balance between acidity and alkalinity measured in the pH value. That is why you want to "cool" your mouth with yoghurt when you have accidentally chewed on a chili pepper. Swedish product developer, Mats Nilsson, learned how to manage fires as a child. His grandfather was a welder at a shipyard. He always had to be careful that he did not burn his shirt while he was working. Grandfather used to drink apple cider during his lunch breaks. Then he noticed that, when he spilled the cider on his shirt and let it dry, that spot would never get burn marks. Mats' grandfather began experimenting with extinguishing fires and involved his grandchildren in his investigations. Mats learned to put out fires shaking a Coca-Cola can and spraying the gas—carbon dioxide—on the fire. The experiment taught him the basics of a modern fire extinguisher that takes away the oxygen and removes the heat of a fire through spraying carbon dioxide on it.

His childhood experiences with his grandfather inspired Mats Nilsson to get his fireman license while he was studying at university. He worked as a fireman for two years before he moved on to a career as product developer. Until, years later, one of his clients—a thermal energy company— asked him to develop a safe, toxic-free, and eco-friendly alternative for existing flame-retardants. Nilsson, who had studied mathematics, physics, chemistry and electronics, and remembered his grandfather's fire lessons, began researching citrus fruit. He knew that lemons have the same cooling effect as yoghurt and stomach acid. People have been eating lemons forever without negative side-effects. Working with natural acids that people have used for thousands of years, seemed a much better idea than gambling on synthetic chemicals with complex names that nobody can remember.

Nilsson experimented and developed a product. However, when he was not yet entirely satisfied and other work came along, the invention ended up on a shelf. That's where it was until, in 2003, Nilsson's wife was looking for an original entry at a Swedish competition for environmentally friendly products. The "nature inspired" Molecular Heat Eater made it to the finals. More praise followed and that led to participation in the BBC World Challenge, a competition for ideas that "really make a difference for the world". To his surprise, Nilsson's innovation also reached the finals of that competition. From there, it went fast. Nilsson refined and completed the product and filed for a patent.

The Molecular Heat Eater, that outperforms chemical flame-retardants in lab tests, comes in a powder, a liquid or a gel. The

exact formulation is a trade secret, but Nilsson is clear that
his product is basically a mix of citrus fruits, grapes, flour and
cellulose. The mixture of bases and acids, that the human body
can easily handle, absorbs the thermal energy, extinguishes the
flames and cools the burning material. Nilsson's invention is, in
scientific terms, a combination of carboxylic acids and inorganic
alkalis that produces a sustainable salt that does not begin to
decompose uncontrollably.

The Molecular Heat Eater is used to treat synthetic materials
like plastics. Nilsson has since also developed another flame-
retardant product, Bio-Eco, that is used to treat natural fiber
materials. This product is, for instance, very successful in
preventing and containing forest fires without polluting the
environment with chemicals. It can also be sprayed on buildings
to protect them from fires.

Nilsson has not yet explored natural alternatives for
other plastic additives beyond flame-retardants. However,
he is convinced that there are natural alternatives for each
problematic artificial solution. UV blockers, for instance, ought
to contain mineral particles, aimed to reflect ultraviolet light
as much as possible. It is possible to create organic salts based
on a chemical reaction between carboxylic acids and minerals
like sodium, potassium, magnesium and calcium. Such a salt
is toxic-free and eco-friendly, and fully degradable in nature.
Or we could get inspiration from the edelweiss flower that is
exposed to excessive sun at high altitudes in the mountains.
The flower disperses UV through thousands of small fibers
rendering the light harmless.

With an eye for nature and a curious mind like Nilsson's,

healthy alternatives for the toxic chemical cocktails that pollute the environment and endanger public health can be (further) developed. The alternatives will be cheaper too, because they can be made from available waste materials in the plant kingdom. According to Nilsson, existing production facilities can be adjusted to new natural flame-retardant substances for a one-time investment of only thousands of dollars. The use of plant waste also means that a natural flame-retardant industry will contribute to reducing carbon emissions.

Nilsson advocates an open source approach and stands ready to share his inventions with any company who wants to produce them, ideally in local production facilities close to the waste materials to speed up their adoption. As global warming seems to lead to an increase in fires in nature around the world, the awareness about entrepreneurial opportunities for natural flame retardants and fire protection should grow. At the same time, a better understanding of plastic pollution and toxic waste may speed up the introduction of cost-effective, toxic-free, eco-friendly, fully in nature degradable plastics and additives that also capture CO_2. Such "healthy" additives would complete and enhance the qualities and uses of the emerging bioplastics as described in the previous chapter.

Chapter 8

Ending plastic pollution: Adding value to waste

It is an unlikely place for a critical innovation transforming the treatment of plastic waste: Compiègne, an hour north of Paris. Compiègne was the site of the train carriage where the historic peace treaty between France and Germany, that ended World War I, was signed. Today, the town has some 40,000 inhabitants, and it is the home of the Technology University of Compiègne. It is here that two students, who received doctorates in chemistry from this university in the 1980s, are revolutionizing the way waste is treated. It was on their door that we knocked in 2016 when we were looking for innovative ways to generate value from plastic waste.

In 1989, Olivier Lepez and Philippe Sajet started a company offering processes for thermo treatment of food products to the food industry. They developed machines to dry, sterilize, roast or cook food items. Some ten years later, they began asking themselves some "environmental" questions. The various processes they were offering to the food industry always produced "leftovers"—waste. As engineers, they knew that waste has a calorific value: there is energy hidden in the molecules. Plastic is made from oil, for instance. From an environmental perspective, it is a waste not to use that energy. Lepez and Sajet adopted the mission of a circular—no waste—economy and added a new service to their ETIA Group portfolio offering methods to turn the waste of industrial food processes into energy—oil or gas.

Their new mission quickly led to a well-known chemical process called pyrolysis. The word comes from ancient Greek: *pyro* means fire and *lysis* means separating. Pyrolysis is a process whereby materials in an oxygen-free environment are being decomposed in new molecules through heat. Because there is no oxygen, the materials are not burning and there is no release of greenhouse gases except for the burning of the fuel to heat the process. The process was used in ancient times to turn wood into charcoal. Today, pyrolysis transforms wood biomass, car tires, plastic, sewage sludge and much more into oil and gas, plus a solid biochar—a type of charcoal used to improve the soil.

The problem with pyrolysis is that the input waste very much determines the quality and consistency of the energy output. It is essential to control the temperature of the process to make sure that you create a regular output. Moreover, materials like plastic turn into a kind of glue in a pyrolysis reactor. It is hard to turn that glue into a consistent quality of oil. That's why plastics first need to be cleaned. The ketchup and the yoghurt need to be removed from the empty containers. The "glue" problem is also a reason that pyrolysis is done in batches so that the reactor can be cleaned after each process. These challenges make pyrolysis a less than perfect solution for processing random and dirty plastic waste in a consistent and continuous process. But that's exactly what the plastic pollution looks like… a messy mix.

Lepez and Sajet studied the pyrolysis process and developed a breakthrough. They built a screw-like conveyor belt that would drive waste in a consistent way through the reactor. The solution solved several problems. There would be no residue anymore that always had to be removed and sometimes even damaged the reactor. It became much easier to control the temperature. The reactor could now also continuously be fed with new waste input enabling the generation of a reliable ongoing energy output. Finally, the technology made it easier to increase the heat in the reactor. That made it possible to crack the waste molecules into an industrial gas mixture called "synthesis gas" or syngas rather than oil. Syngas contains methane, carbon monoxide, carbon dioxide, and hydrogen. That also removed the need to clean plastics before processing saving water, labor and time as the gas molecules simply escape the ketchup et cetera. In the past 16 years, ETIA's "Spirajoule" technology has been installed in some 150 reactors around the world. The technology has been proven. Nevertheless, nobody yet saw the potential for ETIA's "screw" to resolve one of the biggest challenges in the world: plastic pollution.

After Marco Simeoni's "aha!" moment in Rio de Janeiro in 2015, when he realized that the solution to the plastic problem was adding value to the plastic waste, we quickly concluded that turning plastic waste into energy provided the only feasible approach. Let us not forget that all plastics include secret toxic chemical cocktails that must be removed prior to reusing the molecules. For that reason, as we described in chapter 3, given the current production methods of plastics, recycling is unfortunately not yet a realistic option.

We realized that pyrolysis, despite the fact that it is an energy-intensive process, was the only available "war surgery". We started to research providers around the world. We found some 500 companies offering this industrial process. Almost all of them specialize in turning waste into biochar and oil. That was not good enough for us as it means that all plastic would need to be cleaned from food leftovers and more before processing. Cleaning would add one more layer of complexity to the basic infrastructure in the developing countries where 80 percent of the plastic pollution originates. We needed a provider that would be able to turn plastic waste into gas rather than oil, skipping the need for cleaning. The gas would subsequently be sold directly for cooking or heating or used to drive a turbine and generate electricity. As it turned out, there were just 10 providers in the world who offered this "high temperature" (800 degrees centigrade) pyrolysis. Only one of them could offer a continuous process through a remarkable innovation—an essential condition if you want to clean up a lot of waste! Our search ended with ETIA in Compiegne.

The next challenge was to build a small factory that could be easily shipped around the world and that would integrate shredding the plastic waste, transforming that waste into gas through pyrolysis, and finally combusting that gas into electricity. Plastic pollution is a global disaster, but for us it is clear that only small-scale local solutions can solve the problem. The plastic waste has to be processed in the communities that suffer from the pollution and in a way that supports these communities. At our request, ETIA has developed a reactor that fits into eight containers. The Biogreen reactor can be locally installed in four to six weeks on a lot of 1,000 square meters. Depending on the size of the spirajoule, the reactor can process between 1,500 and 4,500 tons of plastic waste per year. In developing countries, that relates to the plastic consumption of at least 50,000 people. Pyrolysis turns that waste into enough energy to support the needs of up to 30,000 people.

The Biogreen reactor is truly "green". The reactor has an advanced filtering system that captures all the toxic gases that are released through the heating of the plastics that contain dangerous additives. That is a major advantage of our approach compared to pyrolysis of plastic waste into oil at lower temperatures (450 degrees). In that case, all the toxins remain in the oil, and that oil should never be burned without putting sophisticated and expensive filters in place. The Biogreen reactor produces 68 percent syngas and 30 percent oil. The fuels can be used directly for cooking, heating, and transportation. They can also be used to power a generator to produce electricity. There is a final two percent of solid waste, char, that can be used for solid fuel, as black carbon or as a filler in concrete.

We decided to concentrate our campaign on Asia where 80 percent of the plastic, that ends up in the oceans, originates. It is estimated that some 12 million tons of plastic were

Photo: © Copyright Louis Villers. Biogreen 300.

Photo: © Copyright Peter Charaf. R4W Biogreen 300. Vernon, France.

dumped in the oceans in 2016. Eighty percent of that would be almost ten million tons. We calculated that to stop all that waste 3,400 Biogreen reactors need to be deployed in Asia in the next ten years. In the process, the campaign will produce clean energy for millions of people.

The technology works, and the calculations of pollution and waste processing match. Our biggest challenge was to develop a business model that would ensure that plastic waste collection and energy production could be done in a sustainable profitable way so that the longevity of the initiative can be guaranteed—more about that in chapter 10. As it turns out, Marco Simeoni's Brazilian aluminum collector is part of global tribe of "waste pickers". It is almost impossible to determine the size of this informal sector in developing countries. They are called *bagerezi* in South Africa; *catadores* in Brazil; and *recicladores* or *cartoneros* in Spanish-speaking countries. A World Bank study once estimated that one to two percent of the global urban population survives by salvaging recyclables from waste. This means that millions of people make a living in the one industry "that is always hiring", collecting and selling materials that someone else has thrown away. In India alone, there are an estimated 1.5 million waste pickers.

A recent study found that in six cities—Cairo (Egypt), Cluj-Napoca (Romania), Lima (Peru), Lusaka (Zambia), Pune (India) and Quezon City (the Philippines)—73,000 people were responsible for recycling three million tons per year. In some countries, waste pickers provide the only form of waste collection and they are responsible for very high recycling rates. In Brazil, for instance, almost 92 percent of aluminum and 80 percent of cardboard is recycled. In Buenos Aires, the cartoneros are on track helping Argentina's capital achieve a "zero garbage" goal.

In 2008, the First World Conference of Waste Pickers was held, confirming the importance of this informal sector in a globalizing world where waste is a fast-growing problem—and opportunity. At present, the waste pickers recycle mostly aluminum, paper and steel. As plastic has no value—with the exception of PET bottles and HDPE canisters —it is not being recycled. Until now.

We started with a test in Iquitos in the Peruvian Amazon. We offered waste pickers who get $0.10 for each kilogram of PET bottles they collect, $0.20 per kilogram for all plastics. The Peruvians collected about 60 kilogram of plastics per person in one day. They made $12 per person, almost three times the local average daily wage. The test clearly showed that plastic collection works when the right incentive is provided. Moreover, the informal waste collection center is well organized. The pickers deliver their waste to "scrap dealers" who sell the collected materials to interested industries. That means that plastic collection can simply be added as a "line item" to existing practices. There is no need to build a new infrastructure.

The informal sector works in a highly efficient way. For example, food multinationals like Danone, Nestlé and Coca-Cola are supporting the recycling of PET bottles in Indonesia. However, they only pay the street collectors for *clean* bottles. As a result, all PET bottles are being delivered clean. Race for Water does not need such precision because the Biogreen reactor can process all plastics as dirty as they are. However, the example underlines that there is an "army" in the world that stands ready to take on the plastic pollution.

The success of the waste collection is first determined by price. A waste picker gets, on average, $0.35 for a kilogram of aluminum, $0.12 for steel and $0.10 for paper. The outcome of our test in Peru at $0.20 per kilogram for all plastic waste was very positive. However, the business model only works sustainably with the right price for the output—energy. If the energy cannot be sold competitively as a gas, fuel or electricity, the collection of plastic waste does not make sense. Our calculations and projections show that we can run a successful business model when we set the fee for the waste picker at $0.15 per kilogram plastic—lower than the test in Iquitos but still higher than what the collectors get for steel and paper; aluminum is in a smaller class of its own. We have also lowered our expectations for the amount of plastic that the waste pickers will collect on a daily basis. Our Peruvian test showed 60 kilograms a day. We calculate that the average waste picker will collect 25 kilograms of plastic per day. If the collectors work 260 days a year, they will turn in 6.5 tons of plastic per person per year.

The economic impact of the program will be phenomenal. We need 1.5 million waste pickers to collect the about 10 million ton of plastic waste that today is still being deposited in the ocean in Asia every year. Their collective annual income will be around $1.5 billion—a massive increase of income that will improve lives and kickstart social and economic development in the poorest communities of developing nations. We can lift people out of poverty!

As long as plastics contain toxic additives, cannot be taken apart again, and there is no reliable model to bring them back to the soil, turning plastics into energy is the best available solution for fighting the pollution. Other initiatives are choosing the same approach confirming the acceptance of the technology. Renewlogy is an initiative from former MIT-students. They have built a plant in Salt Lake City in the United States where plastic is turned into oil through pyrolysis. There is a market: The Earth Institute of Columbia University has estimated that the about 30 million tons of plastic that went into landfills in 2011, could be turned into enough fuel to power nine million cars for a year.

Gasification is a slightly different process to generate value for plastic waste. The process to heat the waste with air or steam, uses a little oxygen but not enough to start combustion. A disadvantage of gasification is that it requires prior cleaning of the plastic waste. The process releases the dangerous toxins of the additives that were used for the plastics. In most cases it is impossible to gasify PVC. And gasification is done in big factories that require significant investments. As a result, the focus is on centralized production with little connection to the needs of local communities. In the United Kingdom, Powerhouse Energy and Waste2Tricity are building a gasification factory to turn plastic waste into hydrogen. This initiative plans to roll out factories in Southeast Asia to clean up plastic pollution.

Despite these initiatives, critics argue that the material efficiency of pyrolysis and gasification is questionable because these are energy-intensive processes. It is true that the economic efficiency is closely related to energy prices. Energy prices, for instance, are on average much lower in the western world. At these prices, our approach with the Biogreen reactor would not be directly competitive for electricity production. We should, however, not forget that the Biogreen solution of Race for Water does not just produces energy, it cleans up the environment as well! Pyrolysis of plastic waste to generate energy is competitive in many situations in developing countries. As we will see in chapter 10, our business model becomes even stronger when we integrate it with a second technology that kickstarts the natural cleanup of the plastic pollution in the oceans and the regeneration of precious marine environments. That is the topic of the next chapter.

A VALUE CHAIN FOR END-OF-LIFE PLASTICS

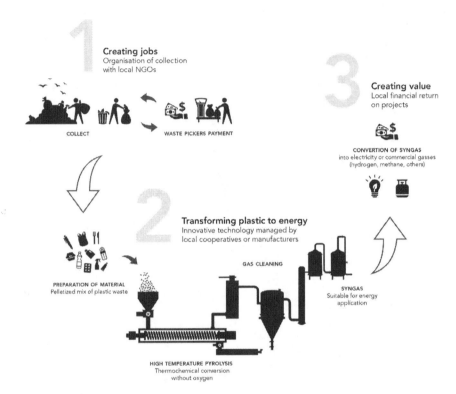

1

Creating jobs
Organisation of collection
with local NGOs

COLLECT

WASTE PICKERS PAYMENT

3

Creating value
Local financial return
on projects

CONVERTION OF SYNGAS
into electricity or commercial gasses
(hydrogen, methane, others)

2

Transforming plastic to energy
Innovative technology managed by
local cooperatives or manufacturers

GAS CLEANING

PREPARATION OF MATERIAL
Pelletized mix of plastic waste

SYNGAS
Suitable for energy
application

HIGH TEMPERATURE PYROLYSIS
Thermochemical conversion
without oxygen

Chapter 9
Nature's response

In the past 200 years, humanity has embarked on a journey that undermines the very foundation of life on Earth. The dinosaurs were wiped out by an asteroid coming from outer space. Humanity is capable of destroying its own future without such outside "support". And yet, while destruction and degradation are happening everywhere, nature is responding. In fact, if humanity would be wiped out today and galactic visitors would arrive here 1,000 years from now, they would find surprisingly little of the damage that humans created.

When you visit an oil refinery and take a sample of the soil that has been polluted for decades, you will find the organisms that are already cleaning up the pollution. The army of these bacteria is too small today to cleanse the environment while the pollution continues. However, left alone for a few centuries or less, they will do the job and our visitors from outer space will have trouble figuring out whatever happened there.

We know that bacteria clean up oil spills that have polluted oceans and beaches. Only years later, it is already hard to find traces of the original pollution that seemed completely devastating when it happened. We think that, when a new and reckless president in Brazil decides to increase tree harvesting in the Amazon, we lose a natural heritage forever. It does not have to be so.

In 1967, Paolo Lugari founded Las Gaviotas, an experimental village in the eastern savannas of Colombia where nobody thought anything could grow after an early group of environmental terrorists, the Spanish *conquistadores*, cut down the last trees 250 years ago. Today, after 50 years and planting some 9 million trees of *one* particular variety on 8,000 hectares, Las Gaviotas sits amidst a reborn rainforest. At the start of the project some 20 species inhabited the devastated land, now researchers count 250 species, as many as in many parts of the Amazon, and that number continues to rise. Lugari offered a little help and nature responded abundantly: Rainforests can be regenerated!

Passionate activists have designed clever structures and technologies attempting to clean up the plastic pollution in the oceans. So far, with very little success. The ocean is just too big, the forces of nature too powerful, and the pollution too widespread. However, what humans cannot do, nature can. In fact, nature is already doing it.

We discovered an emerging solution for the plastic pollution in the oceans by accident. In the past 10 years, scientists and entrepreneurs have increasingly investigated seaweed—or kelp—plantations as sources for food and energy. There are thousands of varieties of seaweeds. They are not affected by the forces of gravity and can grow an astonishing half a meter a day. Our ancestors have cultivated seaweeds for food and fertilizer for centuries. Seaweed contains all essential soil nutrients—natrium, phosphorus, iodine, and potassium—as well as a full range of trace elements. Research suggests that seaweed has been used in China since 2700 BC. In 300 BC, Chi Han wrote a book about seaweed. The Greeks and the Romans used seaweeds as medicine and to feed their animals. However, the practice of harvesting seaweeds was largely abandoned in the 1970s with the arrival of chemical, fossil-fuel based, fertilizers. Only in the Far East, seaweed remained part of the daily diet for humans and animals. However, currently at best 20 percent of the harvested seaweed is being consumed. The remainder is not used and thrown back in the ocean.

Recently, new seaweed pioneers have been experimenting with kelp plantations. In some places they realized harvests of up to 1,000 tons per hectare confirming the massive productivity of seaweeds. However, in other places in similar circumstances—to their surprise—the harvests were not nearly as abundant. When scientists analyzed the seaweeds in their labs, they found a troubling fact. The seaweeds had tiny plastics in their pores that hampered their growth.

Initially, this was bad news. If the seaweeds were growing less, it would decrease the production of biogas and fertilizers, and spoil the emerging new business models. But then we realized that we had stumbled on a most-promising opportunity to design a microplastics capturing system! With a little help, nature can do what it always does: restore and regenerate. And it can do so better than any solely manmade technology. If we plant curtains of seaweed, we know that they will capture the microplastics. We have already established that the microplastics can be captured from the harvested seaweeds. Subsequently, the seaweeds can still be used as intended for food, biogas, fertilizer and much more. The microplastics can be turned into energy through pyrolysis as we have explained in the previous chapter.

A *business model* to clean up the oceans is developing. There is no revenue in the costly attempts to clean up the oceans with heavy, manmade structures and technology. Seaweed, on the other hand, cleans up the ocean *and* provides multiple revenue streams. To understand the business model, we need to study seaweed a bit more. In today's economy we have become used to the concept of externalized *costs*. These are the expenses that society or nature pays for our industrial behavior. The environmental destruction that happens when we mine minerals and that nobody cleans up afterwards is an example of externalized costs. Or, air pollution as a result of the combustion of fossil fuels. Seaweed production, on the other hand, comes with many externalized *benefits*. You read that well: Instead of external costs, this energy and food model generates external benefits while we are also beginning to clean up the oceans.

Recent tests conducted by the Netherlands-based The Seaweed Company off the coast of Ireland demonstrate that one hectare of seaweeds can produce—in two production cycles of six months—a minimum of 200 tons per year. That biomass of 200 tons can be converted in 40,000 cubic meters of gas per year or 110 cubic meters of gas per day for 365 days a year. By comparison, oil companies operating a shale gas field in the United States are happy with on output of 6,000 cubic meters per hour or some 50 million cubic meters per year. However, that field produces gas for only some three to five years before the well is exhausted and nature is left with the damage. Just 1,300 hectares, or 13 square kilometers, of seaweed replaces the production of that shale gas field. Other tests show a seaweed productivity of even up to five times higher which would make the case dramatically more compelling. For the sake of simplicity and transparency, we keep the numbers conservative to manage expectations.

The supply of fossil fuels will end sooner or later. However, seaweed gas can be harvested forever. Investments made today—and maintained over time—will produce *eternal* returns…that is as long as the sun shines and there is water in the ocean. Seaweed gas is a truly clean and renewable resource. The potential of biogas from seaweed is massive. The United States could fulfill its entire annual energy needs with a seaweed ocean farm of 3.3 million square kilometers. That may seem a lot, but farmers cultivate 3.7 million square kilometers of land in the U.S.

The productivity of seaweeds can be explained by the fact that farming in the sea happens in a three-dimensional environment. There are some 12,000 varieties of seaweeds and they grow between three and 25 meters deep. That difference explains the variances in productivity. But all seaweeds grow unaffected by gravity, and that allows for a volume and a speed of conversion of solar energy that are impossible to achieve in farming in a two-dimensional environment on land. In addition, water is 784 times denser than air and supplies a multiple of nutrients. The productivity levels of three-dimensional farming in the sea are beyond the reach of the most advanced attempts to produce food and energy on land with genetically modified organisms (GMOs) and chemical cocktails of fertilizers and pesticides.

The harvested seaweed can be washed to remove the microplastics that got stuck on the outside. Subsequently, the biomass is processed. All the cells are ruptured and start to react with hydrogen in a process known as hydrolysis. That process also allows for the further separation of the microplastics. Subsequently, the biomass can be fermented anaerobically (without oxygen), and new technology makes it possible to efficiently generate methane at scale. Producing biogas through the fermentation of seaweed in a digester is a simple process compared to, for instance, converting corn or sugar cane into ethanol which is a capital-intensive chemical process. The pre-processing of seaweed before the digestion increases the conversion of the biomass into methane (CH_4) and cuts the retention time to about nine days. This increases the efficiency of biomass from the sea compared with any other source with a factor 50. Compared to drilling holes through rocks to find oil wells and gas reserves, working without gravity in a 3D environment is disruptive.

There is another factor that makes seaweed as a source for biogas very compelling: the infrastructure. Most countries already have an infrastructure of natural gas pipelines or bottle distribution. This means that a transition to biogas from seaweeds does not require massive infrastructural investments. A different gas is going to flow through the same pipes or gets pumped into the same portable tanks. That makes seaweed very attractive as a source for power even compared to the rapid rise of wind and solar. Because these stars of the new clean renewable energy world still require quite some investments. Building one large wind turbine requires 900 tons of steel, 2,500 tons of concrete and 45 tons of plastic (!).

The only thing that is required for seaweed biogas is an adaptation of the gas. Experts warn against the corrosive hydrogen sulfide (H_2S) gas that biogas from seaweed contains. That gas may damage pipelines and needs to be taken out. That problem is easily resolved by adding sulfur-loving bacteria in the digestion process of the seaweed. Moreover, shale gas from fracking requires a similar adaptation to be suitable for pipelines.

The environmental impact of seaweed farms is stunning. For example: American fisherman Bren Smith started one of the first commercial 3D ocean farms in the United States. In his book *Eat Like a Fish: My Adventures as a Fisherman Turned Restorative Ocean Farmer*, Smith explains that his "rainforest of the sea" absorbs five times more carbon than land-based plants. He sees himself as a "climate farmer". After a decade of farming, what was once a barren patch of ocean along the coast of Long Island is now a robust ecosystem. The farm system that has won several awards has attracted 150 species that come to hide, eat, and thrive. In addition, the seaweed plantation functions as a storm surge protector, reducing the impact of storms on shoreline communities. While the ecosystem of the oceans is regenerated as on Smith's farm, the beneficial side-effects begin accumulating and new revenue streams emerge. The business model is getting more robust.

After digestion of the seaweed biomass into gas, about three percent of the original weight remains in a solid residue. That byproduct of the digestion is an ideal, phosphates rich, fertilizer. This allows for the reduction and ultimate abandonment of the practice of polluting strip mining of these million years old bird excrements. The seaweed biomass also provides a great source for animal feed: seaweed can replace the soy plantations that have depleted vast areas of agricultural soils for the growing meat consumption.

Livestock contributes as many greenhouse gases as the transportation industry. Nearly 40 percent of that is produced during digestion: cattle, goats, and sheep belch and pass methane, a highly potent greenhouse gas. Studies show that adding a small amount of seaweed to feed of livestock cuts their methane production by nearly 60 percent.

The seaweed production can also be used for additional lucrative business activities. Nearly all processed and frozen foods around the world include seaweed extracts to maintain softness and texture. Seaweed extracts as agar-agar and carrageenan are key ingredients of products like toothpaste, ice cream, and cosmetic creams and lotions.

Seaweed farming can also provide fibers for the textile industry. In the 1940s British scientists already discovered that fibers from seaweeds could be used as non-toxic, non-irritating, biodegradable woven material to treat wounds. Seaweed-based gauze has an anti-inflammatory capacity as well while it maintains a certain degree of humidity which supports wound healing. Since the early 2000s, advanced technologies have introduced seaweed fiber in the production of apparel—mostly in knits, underwear, and sportswear. As the technology improves, seaweed clothing and towels are rapidly arriving as an alternative for cotton that drains water resources and pollutes them with toxins. Note: Cultivating seaweed does not require water. In fact, farming seaweed produces fresh water as byproduct that can be used for irrigation.

European companies, like Landing from Austria, pioneered the seaweed textile technology. But today, China is leading this new industry with the production of millions of units of towels from fibers derived from seaweed. Recently, a Mexican inventor succeeded in producing shoes from recycled plastic bottles with added seaweed. He uses the sargassum seaweed that is threatening the beaches around the Caribbean Sea—as well as the coral reefs—to make the soles.

The most game-changing element of seaweed cultivation is its contribution to the environment. Fracking and fossil fuel exploration *degrade* the environment. These activities are damaging nature. Seaweed cultivation, however, *regenerates* nature. It is very alkaline and maintains the critical pH level in the oceans at 8.2 helping to avert the dangerous drop to 8.1 and below which leads to the destruction of coral reefs and the incapacity of shells to form. Moreover, since dragnet fishing has erased life on the bottom of the sea, there is an urgent need to regenerate the biodiversity of the sea. Once there is an abundance of seaweeds—the precursors of life in the ocean—, sponges and seashells nestle in, fish arrive in a zone where they feel protected from predators. The right conditions to farm oysters, mussels or other crustaceans emerge as well.

As the marine environment regenerates, fish stocks—severely depleted from overfishing—get restored. And the beauty of the three-dimensional ecosystem of the sea is that it does not need any input—irrigation, fertilizers or pesticides. The living organisms feed themselves.

Research shows that seafood is critical for our health. Omega-3 fatty acids from algae—that we can eat directly or through fish, like salmon, anchovies and herring that feed on sea plants too—have been linked in many studies to better brain and heart health. Recently, a Chinese pharmaceutical company introduced a new seaweed-based drug to treat Alzheimer's disease. Chinese scientists had noted the relatively low incidence of Alzheimer's among people who regularly eat seaweed. In trials, the drug shows improvement of cognitive function among people with Alzheimer's in as little as four weeks. The new drug is the first new medicine with the potential to treat the cognitive disorder in 17 years. The innovation illustrates the vast potential for seaweed-related businesses.

Seaweed generates multiple sustainable industries with parallel revenue streams that all operate within the ecosystem. Seaweed cultivation will redesign major sectors of the economy that are trapped in the conventional fossil fuel energy logic. On top of that, seaweed sequesters carbon dioxide. Some varieties absorb five times more CO_2 than land-based plants. If electricity is generated from seaweed, it will only emit 11 grams of carbon per kilowatt-hour whereas the average other energy source for electricity emits more than 500 grams of carbon per kWh.

Given the wide-ranging and compelling advantages of seaweed cultivation, it does not come as a surprise that innovative seaweed initiatives are undertaken around the globe. Indonesia is designing a 100 MW energy plant that will be completely powered by seaweed. Belgium is contemplating seaweed farming as part of a new initiative to protect its coastal zone against climate change. Recently, the U.S. government, after first concluding that a million-dollar subsidy program for the production of ethanol from corn had failed, awarded a series of contracts to stimulate the cultivation of seaweeds for the production of biogas. At the G20 meeting in Osaka in 2019, Japan vowed to spearhead international efforts to tackle plastic waste and the resulting environmental pollution. The Environment Ministry of the Japanese government is delighted with the discovery of the seaweed curtain ocean clean up approach as part of this commitment.

The seaweed story was already a very promising one. And now the opportunity to begin the cleanup of the plastic waste in the oceans is added to this great promise. We have been conducting the first tests to place seaweed "curtains" in shallow coastal zones of up to 25 meters deep. The curtains of 80 by 4 meters that are placed in rows of four gradually block microplastics from reaching the coast. The tests show that the water between the coast and the third curtain is almost plastic free. The objective is to begin cleanup efforts by creating microplastic free zones (MPFZ) around fragile coast lines and preventing small fish, mollusks, oysters and mussels from ingesting microplastics thus stopping it from entering the food chain. Of course, it is essential that no new plastic pollution enters the ocean from land for these MPFZ to emerge. That's why the seaweed curtains have to be created in parallel with the plastic waste capturing system we described in chapter 8.

In the new business model, additional income is generated with each step. The creation of MPFZs opens the door, for instance, to selling premium-priced—microplastic-free (!)—oysters, mussels and other shellfish. And what about the additional value for tourism of swimming in microplastic-free waters?

When the seaweed curtains are harvested, they are placed in a digester and washed with hot water. That process separates the microplastics that can subsequently be processed into energy through pyrolysis (see the previous chapter). Initial tests show that a dense seaweed curtain can capture some 10 billion microparticles per hectare—five kilograms—every six months. Given the amount of plastic pollution in the oceans, these numbers illustrate the extraordinary challenge ahead of us.

In the next ten years with an investment of $12 billion, we envision the establishment of 1,200 square kilometers of seaweed curtains around fragile coastal areas. Of course, this is only a modest beginning. As we discover how efficiently seaweed can capture microplastics, we will need to massively amplify our efforts. We are experimenting with growing curtains with different kinds of seaweeds that can capture different kinds of plastics. We know the concept. However, different seas and different circumstances will require different approaches.

We could make a comparison with the birth of organic agriculture in the 1960s in response to rising concerns at the time about the omnipresence of toxic chemical pesticides. Initially, organic agriculture only made a tiny contribution to food production. Today, organic farming is growing exponentially and, in countries like Italy, Austria, Letland and Estonia, already accounts for more than 10 percent of cultivated lands. Strong forces in Europe strive for 50 percent of all agriculture to be organic. The Indian state of Sikkim has recently declared the region completely organic. The island of Rodrigues of Mauritius is following suit, and major parts of Bhutan are still what they used to be "free of chemical agriculture".

We have to accept that what we polluted in only half a century may take a century or more to be cleaned up. But the time to start is now! The most important fact is that it can be done through an economic process that keeps generating multiple returns and benefits along the way. In the next chapter we are going to run some numbers to illustrate both the vast challenge of the battle eliminating plastic pollution in the oceans as well as what society and planet will gain along the way.

We are standing at the beginning of a huge transformation: a combined revolution of energy production and regeneration of the oceans. Seaweed cultivation does not compare with anything that we have. It will inspire generations of scientists and entrepreneurs to come with opportunities to fuel and feed societies in sustainable and renewable ways while cleaning up the mess that we should never have created.

Chapter 10

1 + 1 = 3: A system with multiple benefits

Wolves changes the course of rivers. It is one of those examples of the magic of the complexity of nature. It is a story that shows how the linear, one-dimensional approach of humans often fails to produce the best results with the most benefits for all. In nature, 1 + 1 = always at least 3. And that's why the story of the wolves and the rivers is relevant to make sure that our plastic pollution strategy is most effective.

In the beginning of the 20th century, the United States established many national parks under the authority of a National Park Service (NPS) to preserve America's nature and wilderness. The NPS concluded at the time that the wolf posed a threat to wildlife. Hunters were given permission to shoot them. As a result, the last wolf was killed in Yellowstone Park in 1926. Twenty-five years ago, as new ecological wisdom had emerged, the park authorities decided to reintroduce the wolf. A few years ago, when they analyzed the impact of the return of the wolves, scientists concluded—as expected—that the populations of elk and deer had diminished. But the scientists also determined that the reintroduction of the wolves had changed the course of rivers and creeks in Yellowstone.

Here's their analysis: with the return of the wolf, deer and elk began to avoid the exposed banks along rivers and creeks. They made sure they protected themselves from the predators in the forests. As a result, the vegetation along the rivers expanded. This changed the course of the water flows. That may not seem so important. However, the vegetation along rivers provides a rich habitat for many species that make a thriving ecosystem. In other words: the wolf is not a threat to wildlife; it is part of a healthy ecosystem. Without the wolf the ecosystem was compromised.

The story of the return of the wolf in Yellowstone Park illustrates that when you bring elements together, a system will emerge: The more diversity, the more resilience, the more effective water, nutrients, energy and matter are being distributed and used. The new system somehow holds properties that do not exist in the separate elements that form the system. For example, if you take all the parts of a watch and lay them out on the table, they will not tell the time the way an assembled watch does. If you take all the pieces of a flower and lay them on the ground, they will not grow and flourish the way a whole flower does. You can also say that when quantity increases—more elements come together— quality changes.

We have introduced two well-known technologies in this book: pyrolysis and digestion. Both these technologies are the subject of substantial criticism that has, so far, prevented their widespread acceptance. We argue that pyrolysis is the only available technology that we can use to transform—and eliminate—all types of plastic waste. Critics object that pyrolysis is energy-intensive and expensive. Therefore, they say, it is not a viable technology, and they miss the point that we are primarily presenting pyrolysis to get rid of plastic waste, not because it is the best way to produce energy.

Similarly, digestion of seaweed is criticized because the technology cannot be easily standardized and, consequently, is unpredictable. Different seaweeds have different compositions and therefore different outputs. Both criticisms come from the same linear thinking that led to the initial extinction of the wolf in Yellowstone Park.

Just as in nature, opportunities arise when we bring elements together. First: our approach is decentralized and focused on responding to local needs and opportunities. In some places the focus will be to produce electricity with the syngas made in the pyrolysis reactor, because the local community needs that electricity. In other places, we will directly sell bottled gas because that fills a local need. There will be communities—far away from the coasts—that suffer from plastic pollution where we create employment and clean up the pollution through placing pyrolysis reactors but where we cannot start seaweed plantations. In short: we implement plastic solutions. Plural—not one size fits all.

Even so, our vision is to combine the traditional technologies of pyrolysis and digestion in an innovative, revolutionary new way. As we shall see, the combination leads to an exponential improvement of our business model. We will explain the opportunity with a little chemistry.

In a biodigester, biomass is fermented into gases and a solid residue sludge. This happens in an oxygen-free, anaerobe environment. Half the biomass consists of water, H_2O, the half consists mostly of carbon, the "C" of the periodic table. In the digestion, the C's combine with the H's and form CH_4, or methane gas, that can be burned. The efficiency of the process of producing CH_4 is limited by the number of hydrogen (H) atoms that are available. As there are four H's needed to bond with one C atom to form one CH_4 molecule, the biomass can at most be converted into 50 percent methane gas. There are not enough H atoms available to form more CH_4 molecules. The remainder—some 40 percent—of the available C atoms combine with oxygen into carbon dioxide (CO_2), the greenhouse gas we do not want. Finally, the fermentation leads to a few percent hydrogen sulfide (H_2S) and some five percent sludge.

Now, let's look at the pyrolysis reactor. Under high heat, plastics are transformed into a syn(thetic) gas. This syngas consist of up to 30 percent hydrogen, 50 percent methane with a remainder of 16 percent ethylene (C_2H_4) and 2 percent poisonous carbon monoxide (CO) and 2 percent carbon dioxide (CO_2). A fraction is converted into fuel like diesel and gas, and a few percent solid waste remains that contains all the harmful pollutants in the plastic as well as the biological remains. This waste is sent to a cement plant where it is fully destructed in the process of producing cement.

A breakthrough opportunity arises when we feed the hydrogen-rich syngas from the pyrolysis reactor into the biodigester. More hydrogen means that more H atoms are available to convert biomass into methane gas. If we combine the two technologies, we can turn the biomass into more than 90 percent CH_4. That means we are increasing the efficiency of the biodigester from 50 to 90 percent, or with 80 percent. We also increase the mineralization of the process which leads to a better quality of phosphate fertilizer. Furthermore, the increased mineralization in the biodigester makes it easier to separate the plastic microparticles from the seaweed. And these particles are now fed back into the pyrolysis reactor for their final destruction. Pyrolysis of microplastics captured with seaweed curtains alone is too expensive. The introduction of microplastics with biological residues into an existing pyrolysis makes economic sense. The integration of two systems multiplies the efficiencies.

Here's the inspiring and powerful emerging business model. We need $12 billion to place 3,400 pyrolysis reactors in coastal communities in Southeast Asia (see chapter 8). We need an additional $12 billion to establish some 35 hectares of Microplastic Free Zones in front of the coastlines of each of these 3,400 communities. That means we are going to start 120,000 hectares or 1,200 square kilometers of seaweed plantations (see chapter 9).

A total investment of $24 billion may seem like a lot of money. Let us put that number in perspective: The cost of generating one gigawatt with nuclear power is about $4 billion. That means we can clean up plastic pollution, develop communities and regenerate oceans for the same amount of money as needed for building one nuclear power station that generates six gigawatts! Such a nuclear power plant is smaller than existing nuclear power stations in Japan, South Korea, China and Canada.

The seaweed plantations require a digester facility on land that will transform the seaweed biomass into biogas. These digesters will be set up in connection with the pyrolysis reactors. As outlined above, the syngas of the pyrolysis reactors will be fed into the digester to substantially improve the output of the seaweed digestion.

As we laid out in chapter 9, we conservatively project the annual harvest of seaweed at 200 tons per hectare—some tests show up to 1,000 tons per hectare, or five times as much. The total annual harvest of the 1,200 square kilometers seaweed plantations will be 24 million tons. With the support of the hydrogen in the syngas from the pyrolysis we can turn a ton of seaweed into 36 cubic meters of biogas. That means that 24 million tons of seaweed will be transformed into 864 million cubic meters of gas per year.

Now we add the 50 percent methane from the pyrolysis syngas: 4,091 million cubic meters. That leads to a total volume of methane gas of 4,955 million cubic meters. The price for one cubic meter of bottled gas in developing markets is about $1 bringing the total value of our annual biogas production to $4,955 million.

The digester also leaves a solid residue that is rich in phosphates and iodine—an ideal fertilizer. The residue is about three percent of the original seaweed volume of 24 million tons. That means that digestion gives us 720,000 tons of bio fertilizer per year. The market value of that fertilizer is $150 per ton: we add $108 million per year to our revenue.

The next main revenue source comes from selling the carbon sequestration rights. Twenty-four million tons of seaweed captures 48 million tons of carbon-dioxide. In Asia, the price for carbon sequestration lies at $5 per ton. This adds another $240 million to our annual revenue stream.

Our "plastic solutions" enterprise is making $5,303 million per year and we are not counting the multiple additional cash benefits that seaweed cultivation provides. From fibers for the textile industry to supplements that reduce the methane production of cows, and from Alzheimer drugs and ingredients for the food and cosmetics industries to higher prices for "plastic free" oysters and beach tourism, there are many supplemental sources of revenue. Please note a critical strength of our business model: the multitude of cash flows reduces the risks within the whole system.

The operating expenses of the pyrolysis reactors and the digesters as well as the pay for 1.5 million trash collectors require $4,090 million per year. That means that we project an annual cash income of $1,213 million or a 5 percent annual return on the investment of $24 billion. We have a business!

But let's take a closer look at what we are actually doing. We are not just stopping the dumping of 80 percent of all plastic waste in the oceans. We are also beginning to regenerate the oceans. What is the value, a decade from now, from the fact that small fish will be better protected in the seaweed forests of our microplastic free zones? What does it mean, a hundred years from now, that fish stocks have been replenished for the half of the world population that depends on seafood protein on a daily basis?

From the perspective of future generations, resolving the plastic pollution in the oceans is a project with a massive return. Just think what it means when 1.5 million poor trash collectors are going to generate an income of $1.5 billion! New homes will be built, new schools and businesses will be started, and communities and societies will be transformed for these people. At the same time, the impact on the environment is massive as well. In May 2019, a group of scientists from the Plymouth Marine Laboratory published a first study attempting to quantify the global ecological, social and economic impacts of the plastic pollution in the oceans. The study concludes that the plastic waste in the oceans has an annual cost of $2,500 billion or $33,000 per ton that is dumped. That also means that if we prevent 10 million tons of plastic to get into the ocean, we are saving $330 billion *each year*. Remember: our *initial* investment is only $24 billion! As our model evolves and improves, we will continue to invest. We will continue to clean up the oceans and restore marine ecosystems, while we continue to make money.

There are more environmental savings. Waste companies pay $95 per ton to dump waste in landfills. Our informal trash collectors prevent the institutional collection of 9.6 million tons of waste. That saves almost $1 billion per year. At the same time, when we sell gas and electricity, we replace the need for diesel fuel. The estimated annual savings of that substitution are $650 million.

Local governments, that often spend 10 percent or more of their budgets on fuel subsidies, benefit from the projected savings in diesel consumption and waste management.

That would make them a good candidate for funding our enterprises. At the same time, governments are notoriously cash-poor in developing countries. In many cases, governments do not save money on waste management as the waste is not even collected at the moment. According to The Organization for Economic Co-operation and Development (OECD), two billion people in the world have no access to waste management. That also means that local authorities have no budget allocated to dealing with plastic waste.

From a macro perspective—including the needs and interests of planet and society—our model is very efficient and even lucrative. From a micro perspective—only including direct revenue and expenses—it is a challenge to finance. We need other investors. Given the fact that public awareness of the threats and dangers of plastic pollution has increased substantially in recent years, institutions like the World Bank, that do not need to follow strict market investment rules, should step in. Alternatively, it makes a lot of sense for major plastic polluters, like soft drink companies and other packaged goods multinationals, to guarantee bank loans to fund this initiative. These companies clearly bear responsibility for the pollution and—in this way—can help clean up their mess through a profitable business.

There are recent signs of a positive responses to the challenge by these corporations. In October 2018, the European Investment Bank (EIB) launched the Clean Oceans Initiative jointly with the KfW group and the Agence Française de Développement. Together, these three banks will provide up to €2 billion in lending over the next five years to support projects that collect plastics and clean up wastewater before it reaches the ocean. In 2019, The Alliance to End Plastic Waste was founded. This alliance brings together many leading multinationals that are active in the plastics and consumer goods value chain: BASF, Berry Global, Braskem, Chevron Phillips Chemical Company LLC, Clariant, Covestro, Dow, DSM, Exxon Mobil, Formosa Plastics Corporation USA, Henkel, Lyondell Basell, Mitsubishi Chemical Holdings, Mitsui Chemicals, NOVA Chemicals, OxyChem, PolyOne, Procter & Gamble, Reliance Industries, SABIC, Sasol, SUEZ, Shell, SCG Chemicals, Sumitomo Chemical, Total, Veolia, and Versalis. The initiative has committed over $1.5 billion over the next five years to help end plastic waste in the environment.

Ultimately, our plastic solutions call for a different type of investor: the one who believes that we need to invest for the benefit of future generations and that we have a shared responsibility to clean up the mess we have created. Let's be clear: we are cleaning up plastic pollution, regenerating oceans, creating jobs in developing countries while making money. Few "impact" investment opportunities come close to such major, long-term, world-changing effects. There are investors who see this opportunity and we will set the stage for them in the final chapter.

With great gratitude to Johan Manuel Redondo, PhD and Danny W. Ibarra of the University of Bogota, Colombia, on whose projections and modeling most of this chapter is based. See Annex for further details.

Chapter 11

A 100 year vision: An opportunity for captains of legacy

While you are reading this page...
   ... the equivalent of another truck load of plastic waste is dumped in the ocean;
   ... a gust of wind is carrying plastic microparticles to another untouched, pristine place on the planet;
   ... an inadequate recycling facility in a developing country is burning plastic waste in the open air releasing toxic black smoke into a poor community...
   We have to be realistic: the cleanup of plastic pollution around the world is a gigantic challenge. Even if we are able, in the next six to ten years with a $12 billion investment, to stop 80 percent of the plastic waste going into the ocean in Southeast Asia through strategically placing more than 3,000 "waste to energy" container factories, we will still be facing the reality that oceans, mountains and deserts around the world will be full of (micro)plastics. If we add another $12 billion to plant the first 1,200 square kilometers of seaweed curtains, we are only beginning the regeneration of the oceans. At the current rate of capturing 5 kilograms plastic microparticles per

hectare per year with planting seaweed curtains, we should not even begin to calculate how much seaweed we exactly need to plant, harvest, and process to make the oceans clean again.

However, we have to be realistic about something else too: human history is full of "impossible" achievements. Again, and again, humans have been able to turn incredible visions into practical realities. We should remind ourselves that each artifact in our home, office or school was first imagined as part of fantasy. The first landing on the moon was the result of such a vision. One simple fact illustrates the improbability of that mission: the iPhone in your pocket has over 100,000 times the processing power of the computer that landed man on the moon 50 years ago. Who could "realistically" believe John F. Kennedy when he said in 1961 that man would walk on the moon within a decade?

Compared to landing on the moon, getting rid of plastic pollution on planet Earth is not a 10-year vision. We cannot restore in years what was dumped into the environment in half a century. Today, we present a 100-year vision. Placing the first Biogreen reactors and planting the first seaweed curtains, are only the first steps of a very long journey. But that journey can and will be successful with a strong business model supported by the power of nature. That is the force of our vision. Soon, every minute while the pollution continues, we will also create new jobs, restore environments and make money.

A flywheel of cascading positive developments will begin to turn. Driven by a good business model, small steps will become bigger steps. Further innovation will improve the business case. Guided by the first experiences in the field quickly moving from curtains of hundreds of meters to curtains of hundreds of kilometers, and then to forests of millions of square kilometers, we will find ways for seaweed to capture more microplastics. While we embrace fully degradable bioplastics and deal with additives, nature will find ways to clear deserts and mountains of the pollution we created. Remember: the bacteria we need are already alive and present in the soil, the air and the oceans! It IS realistic to clean the plastic pollution in the world in 100 years.

We are confident because we know that there is no more powerful force to drive innovation and change than human enterprise. Governments can have a big impact and facilitate and support outcomes for the common good through regulation and tax policies. However, policy makers often manage conflicting interests. They suffer from aggressive lobbyists, are influenced by the short-term impact of the next election, and therefore hesitate to make the bold decisions that are required. In the end, only enterprising pioneers and impact investors lead fundamental innovation over generations. There is a good reason for that. No initiative can ever sustain social and environmental goals over time unless it is assured of a continuous flow of revenue and the building up of financial— and social—capital. If critical social and environmental initiatives depend on subsidies or charity, they are at permanent risk and will likely face disruptions.

We face a challenge, however. As we have seen, business as we know it today has become a force that serves only a few at the expense of many and of the environment on which all life depends. While we were writing this book, Royal Dutch

Shell was building a giant new factory 150 hectares bordering the Ohio river outside Pittsburgh in the United States. The factory will produce more than a million tons of tiny plastic pellets a year that can be turned into items like phone cases, auto parts and food packaging. And, as we know, these pellets are not (yet) designed to degrade in soil, sun and sea, and will be around for centuries after these products have served their purpose. As proof that politicians are not standing up to protect the interests of planet and people, Shell got a tax break that is projected to save the company an estimated $1.6 billion in the years ahead. And, yes, the factory will provide 5,000 jobs.

The reality is that—if left alone—business often does not serve the interests of people and planet. The prevailing logic is that a business must first serve the shareholder. In many cases, even if business does not cause direct harm, it does not serve the common good either. Business often contributes to a breakdown of the very critical social tissue that holds society together.

Some of the highest entrepreneurial achievements today are initiatives—like Facebook, Airbnb, and Uber—that create billions for a few people out of services that do not respond to the most basic needs of communities around the world. Uber neglects the social safety of drivers and passengers and the presence of Airbnb is creating affordable housing shortages for lower- and middle-income families including students. In the past, steel and railway barons also became extremely wealthy, but their contributions were arguably much more related to common interests and needs.

We have even invented a new category of business to

describe activities that support society at large. We talk about "responsible business" and "social entrepreneurs." These terms reflect great initiatives, but like the non-profits, they haven't had a major impact on changing the overall negative and destructive course that business is on in today's world. Moreover, "responsible business" and "social entrepreneurs" sound like "organic apples". In the strange world we are living in, it has become normal to treat fruits like apples with all kinds of artificial, unhealthy substances to "protect" them against insects, etc. And as a result, there are also people growing natural apples that we call "organic apples". We have given a new name to something that was always there: An apple that falls from a tree is, well… an apple. Shouldn't we instead have given that new treated apple its own name—a "chemical" apple?

Similarly, there is only one objective for business: to provide products and services to serve the interests of society and to create value for society. That's why corporations receive a license to operate. Instead of calling businesses that serve the common good "responsible" or "social," we should call the degenerated version of modern business today "irresponsible" or "destructive" business. There is power in words. They help us understand what we are doing.

The corporation, as we know it, was a clever Dutch invention. The world's first multinational was Holland's Vereenigde Oostindische Compagnie (VOC, or Dutch East India Company), founded in 1602. Dutch merchants had discovered they needed more investments to finance risky trade expeditions to Asia. Up to that time, companies were partnerships. The people involved in a firm made joint investments and ran their company together. Managers and owners were one and the same. That concept constrained the size of investments: there was a limit to the number of partners who could successfully work together. The new model created by Dutch tradesmen involved detaching the company's ownership and management. There were shareholders, who invested money but didn't go to sea and weren't involved in other dealings of the company. Thanks to this structure, the Dutch VOC was able to raise a lot more money from a greater number of people to pursue its activities.

But there was one obstacle. The expeditions the company embarked upon were high risk, comparable in our era to space exploration. Ships often sank during the lengthy voyages. In other words, major investments could be easily lost and—even worse—shareholders could be held liable for big losses when a storm in the Pacific or a pirate raid meant suppliers couldn't be paid or a shipment didn't make it to buyers. At that time, it was commonplace to transfer debts from one generation to the next until they were settled.

This practice severely curtailed investments. Shareholders weren't terribly enthusiastic about investing in companies in which they had no influence and that could burden them—and their offspring—with debts. VOC's solution? Limited liability. Investors and shareholders could never lose more than their investment. And that creative and lucrative system, marked by a limited risk of loss and an unlimited opportunity for profit, still exists today—with huge consequences for all of society.

In the colonial era, such "corporate egotism" served a general, public interest. Plundering of colonies was considered to be in the general interest of prosperity of the colonizing power— the fact that this was a reprehensible vision is another story. The government granted companies like the Dutch VOC the right to confer limited liability on their shareholders as long as it was clear that the company served the public interest. The worst risk back then was a sunken or seized ship, and the limited liability of shareholders involved financial debt.

Nowadays there are significant other interests at stake— including environmental and public health. Plastic production affects generations to come. It may take more than a century to get all the plastic waste out the oceans again. The toxic additives in plastic end up in the food chain. It is not just plastic. Pharmaceutical manufacturers introduce powerful medicines on the market that will have consequences 100 years from now. Ingredients remain active long after pills have been taken. Antibiotics continue to "treat" flora, fauna and our gut far beyond the prescription. Tanker ships carrying oil or chemicals can destroy natural areas for decades. Dangerous nuclear power and chemical plants are located near densely populated cities, where mistakes can quickly turn into full-scale disaster. It is not at all clear that all these activities serve the public interest and the common good.

The Dutch VOC executives had to negotiate with the government— representing the public interest—to get their license that would give their corporation limited liability. The license was a privilege that was granted by the representatives of the people to an initiative that was perceived to have the public's best interests in mind. That is very different today.

Anyone can set up a limited liability company by simply filling out a form and paying a registration fee. The days are long gone that business owners had to negotiate with the authorities regarding what would be done in return for the right to limited liability. Nobody who launches a corporation today feels he is granted a special privilege, and nobody acts accordingly. In fact, today, businesses only negotiate with governments about subsidies and tax benefits in return for their investments.

Nobody asks whether Monsanto should get a license to produce the pesticide glyphosate, which is classified by reputable organizations as a possible carcinogen? Or, should Shell get a license to build a factory to produce millions of tons of a substance that we know will endanger public health and pollute the environment for decades if not centuries?

We may have to wait a long time before the mainstream world of government and business redesigns the rules of the business game so that the corporate world will serve society again. However, we cannot afford to wait for the necessary consensus to emerge to stop and clean up the plastic pollution around the world. We cannot stop the plastic pollution with "business as usual", but we can solve it with *business*. We can solve plastics crisis with business models that can stand rigorous accounting analysis. But these models need visionary support.

In the late 19th century, when the Industrial Revolution was well underway, a new term was introduced to describe entrepreneurs who not only served their personal financial interests but also contributed positively to society in some way.

The "captains of industry" earned the respect that eluded the "robber barons" of the time. As we have discovered, there is no quick fix to clean up the plastic pollution. We are going to need time and persistent dedication to meet the challenge. We need a long-term vision focused on the health of people and planet. That is why we need a new tribe: Captains of Legacy. Captains of Legacy are entrepreneurs and investors who are not afraid to start a journey while they themselves may never see the destination. But, as Ralph Waldo Emerson said it so well: "It is not the destination, it is the journey". And the journey can be a fruitful and profitable one.

You hardly create a meaningful legacy when you develop a carcinogenic plastic, make a few billions from it, and then give it away to good causes. How much sense does it make to make a fortune on ripping the earth and then donate a part of what you earned to alleviate the pain caused? Captains of Legacy do not make money the *wrong* way to give it back the *right* way. Captains of Legacy give their best creative energy to transforming the world toward a better society, working in harmony with nature; they are dedicated to doing much better all the time. While doing so over time, they will make money, and their children and grandchildren may even make a lot of money, and there is nothing wrong with that. However, their first priority is always meeting the needs of society—alleviating poverty, generating jobs, restoring nature.

Let's be careful with the word legacy. The legacy does not have to be one great invention—a plastic bag that degrades in sun, water and soil—or one big industry. A legacy can be an idea, an approach that leads to transformation—turning plastic waste into electricity or farming seaweed to capture microplastics—that can be copied by millions around the globe. A new generation of millennials is making clear on a daily basis that they stand ready to contribute in a different way than their parents. They are natural members of the new tribe of captains of legacy.

To get them going—as well as anyone who wants to contribute to putting communities and nature back on their evolutionary paths—we first need to remove possibly the biggest obstacle that stands in the way of the success of the new tribe: the master's degree in business administration or MBA. It has become common practice to teach entrepreneurs the writing of a business plan, the capacity to present the 30-second elevator pitch, the ability to enforce management by objectives, to undertake market analysis, exercise the transparency of budget controls, the discipline of strategic planning, and, of course, financial analysis, including investment options and fundraising techniques. All of this jargon may be useful if you want to manage a multinational corporation with a global reach, and the ultimate goal is to cut costs through imposing economies of scale and rigid supply-chain management in a "one size fits all" model. However, this "MBA-speak" is totally ineffective if we wish to serve the basic needs in societies.

Yvon Chouinard, founder of outdoor gear manufacturer Patagonia, arguably the most successful sustainable enterprise in the textile industry, never went to college and started his company to provide climbing gear for his friends so that he himself would have money to go rock climbing as well. Chouinard responded to a need… In fact, it is exactly because we enforce the MBA doctrine on entrepreneurs that thousands of initiatives undertaken by civil society over a quarter of a century with ample funding have not been able to fundamentally change reality—that is: They have not erased widespread poverty, hunger and malnutrition, and environmental degradation.

The fundamental flaw is this: We cannot subject and limit entrepreneurship to managerial techniques. Entrepreneurship is in the first place about identifying and responding to needs. That requires an ability to get out of the box and navigate unchartered environments. Turning plastic waste into energy through high temperature pyrolysis is a tested technology, and growing seaweeds is a century old practice. However, to use pyrolysis in a few thousand mini factories in complex urban settings, requires ongoing flexibility and a preparedness to adapt and change along the way. Similarly, planting seaweed curtains across the coastal areas of the planet needs ongoing adaptation. Communities have different local customs and different local needs. Communities may also present new opportunities to fulfill needs that will further strengthen local business.

Building mini factories with roots in communities that provide energy and jobs for these communities requires a very different vision and approach than "rolling out" a business concept through a tested franchise model. There are some 37,000 McDonald's locations in the world, which serve 68 million people every day. It took 70 years to build the company to what it is today. It may seem impressive, but there are 800 million people suffering from malnutrition worldwide. The McDonald's model—irrespective of the quality of the fast food and its devastating impact by spreading cattle farming on cleared rainforests—is clearly not going to solve that problem anytime soon. With that kind of entrepreneurship, we are not going to solve the problem of plastic waste, neither of hunger and poverty.

Establishing seaweed plantations in the oceans around the world means working closely with nature in ever-changing circumstances. Today, we know that certain seaweeds capture plastic micro particles while they provide biomass for energy and food. The seaweeds also provide valuable ingredients for the cosmetics and bioplastics industries. They restore the marine environment and fish stocks. Seaweeds may provide many more benefits that we do not yet observe. They may also pose challenges that we haven't discovered yet. Growing seaweeds is going to be a dance with nature. That dance will follow the core principle of nature: there is always an abundance of resources and opportunities. It is a reality that sharply contrasts with the scarcity that traditional economics teaches. Actually, the strategy of farming millions of tons of seaweed may get us to a "strange" concept in economics: abundance.

Nature keeps evolving, responding and filling new niches. Modern science is continuously catching up. Remember that we found the opportunity to clean the oceans with seaweeds by accident. Remember that, for a long time, we misread the history of Rapa Nui. As evolution continues, it is of great importance to keep continuously discovering and exploring.

The hardest thing for an entrepreneur, for a Captain of Legacy,—indeed for any human being—is to always maintain a beginner's mind. The current project may very well be only the small steppingstone to a next step that is bigger and more impactful than you can imagine today. But you can only find that next bigger opportunity when you are not too fixated on what you have at hand. Over time—when understanding of natural processes increases— this systems approach to enterprise will become a second nature.

We have not made enough progress in solving the problem of plastics pollution yet, because that challenge does not easily fit in any existing MBA-inspired business plan or strategy. As incredible as that sounds, Shell is not in the "cleaning up the plastics" industry. Nor are they designing new polymers that will degrade in sun, soil and sea! The food and other multinationals that happily use plastics to package their goods are not any closer to redesigning the "throwaway products logic" either. The core business policies are not directed at cycling raw materials back to the soil. The early attempts to introduce circular economy practices are not changing the direction of the statistics.

We stand at a critical juncture where only a new tribe of Captains of Legacy can make sure that we do the things that need to be done to preserve the future for generations to come. It took 40 years to restore the rainforest in Las Gaviotas to the level it is at today. It may take even longer to establish seaweed plantations around the world. However, planting seaweed is surely easier and will mean more for future inhabitants of this planet than plotting traveling to Mars some

225 million kilometers away—and that is a venture that many of today's billionaires are actively supporting.

And is time a problem? Many travelers are inspired when they visit the medieval cathedrals spread around the countries of Europe. Most of them were built over more than a century. This means that the visionary leaders who were determined to endow their cities with cathedrals would never see their final works of art and architecture, and they knew it. And the carpenters and sculptors knew that they were not going to enjoy the finished results of their work during their lifetimes. Still, everyone believed in the project and was inspired and motivated to contribute their money and talents for a few generations to come. That is the role and the responsibility of the Captain of Legacy.

After decades of plastic pollution and destruction of nature, the process of cleaning up and restoration will be like building cathedrals. We need Captains of Legacy who, like the cathedral carpenters, believe that you can change the course of our society and reestablish harmony with the planet.

And, what about *you*?

You may not be a legacy investor, but you are part of the global plastic solutions movement, too. There is a lesser known part of the first man on the moon story. Sometime after his speech to the U.S. Congress, president Kennedy brought a visiting foreign dignitary to the NASA headquarters. When they passed a man sweeping the floor in a hallway, the guest shakes the man's hand and asks: "What are you doing here?" The cleaner replies: "We are going to put a man on the moon!"

You can help increasing the awareness that we have a

business model to clean up the plastic pollution.

Perhaps you can bring your community together and buy a Biogreen reactor to create the first plastic waste free town.

Or, you can spread the story of the fully degradable plastics of Italian manufacturer Novamont (by the way: Novamont stands ready to share its innovation to make sure that degradable bioplastics can quickly spread around the world).

You can make sure that you only use glass bottles and containers.

You can pass on this book so that the movement grows and finds the resources it needs.

As every business knows, the consumer has the ultimate power.

With vision, commitment, and a business model we will clean up the plastic pollution. Yes, it will take time, but the journey will be meaningful and rewarding from the start. And, remember, the impossible is just something that has not happened yet.

Are you ready?

Resources

Race for Water Foundation: https://www.raceforwater.org/
The Blue Economy: https://www.theblueeconomy.org/
Zero Emission and Research Initiative: http://www.zeri.org/
Kamp Solutions Magazine: https://kamp.solutions/
Novamont: https://www.novamont.com/
Dycle: https://dycle.org/
Trulstech: https://www.trulstech.org/

Annex

The Release Of Microplastics (1)

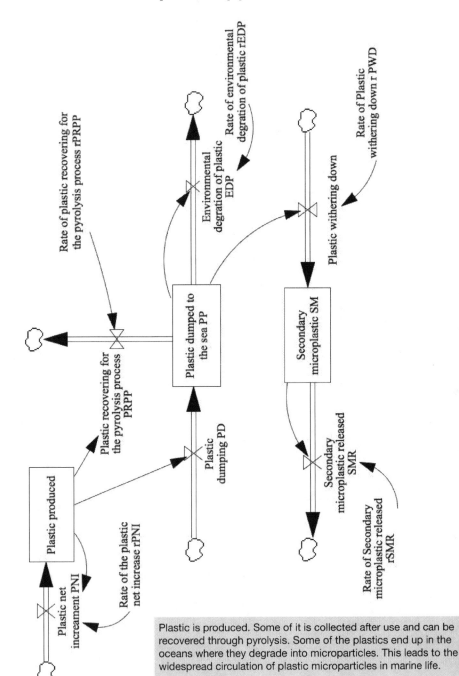

Plastic is produced. Some of it is collected after use and can be recovered through pyrolysis. Some of the plastics end up in the oceans where they degrade into microparticles. This leads to the widespread circulation of plastic microparticles in marine life.

The Release Of Microplastics (2)

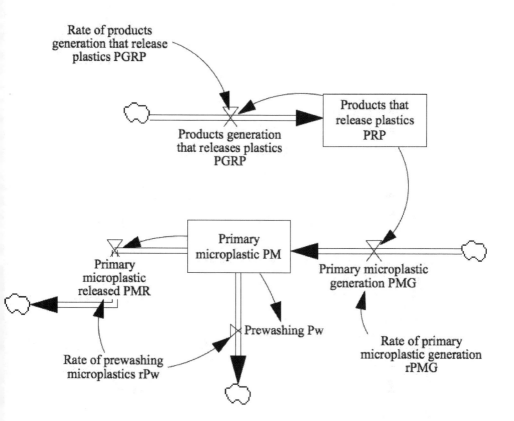

The release of microplastics is beyond control. There is primary microplastic release. Some plastics are designed to be tiny, and there are big pieces that are weathered into tiny ones. The second major source of microplastics in the environment comes from products—from clothing to toys—that release plastic microparticles during their lifetime.

Capturing Microplastics Through Seaweed Farms

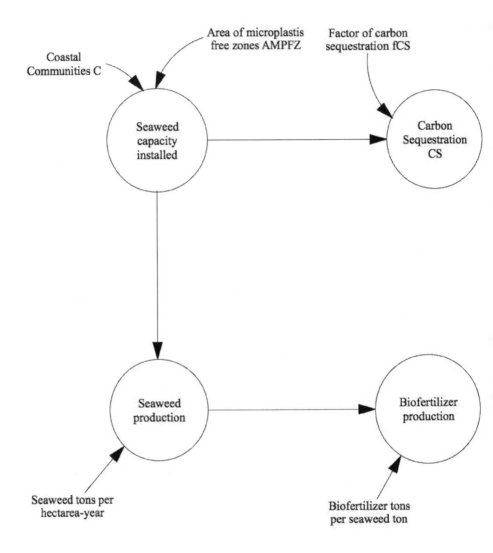

We need a model that generates a revenue while offering solutions to the errors of the past, and ensure that there is a clear benefit for the local communities. Seaweed "curtains" in front of the coast capture plastic microparticles. The seaweed production comes with many additional benefits: biogas, carbon sequestration, fertilizer and more.

Turning Plastic Waste Into Energy

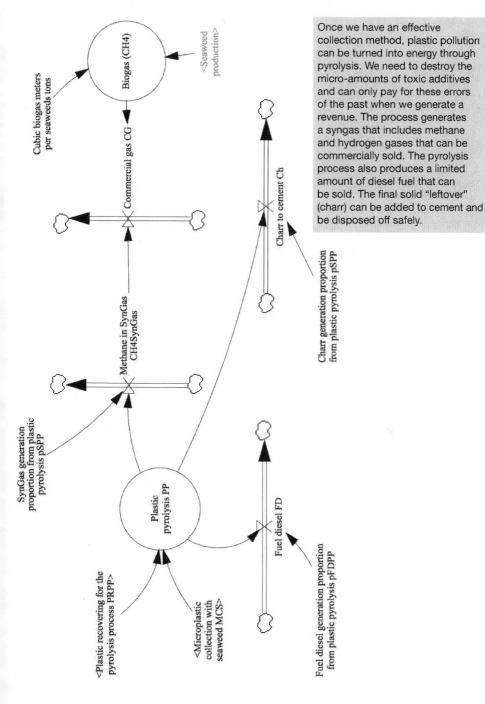

Once we have an effective collection method, plastic pollution can be turned into energy through pyrolysis. We need to destroy the micro-amounts of toxic additives and can only pay for these errors of the past when we generate a revenue. The process generates a syngas that includes methane and hydrogen gases that can be commercially sold. The pyrolysis process also produces a limited amount of diesel fuel that can be sold. The final solid "leftover" (charr) can be added to cement and be disposed off safely.

The Dynamics Of Microplastics And Collection

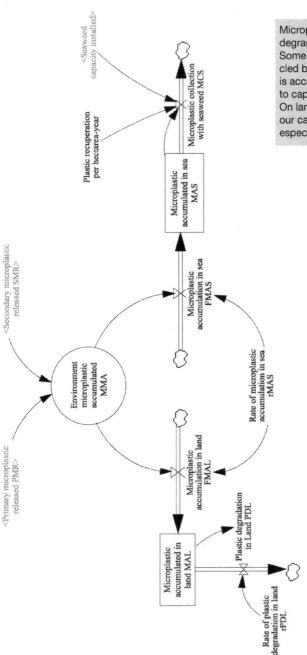

Microplastics accumulate and degrade on land and in the oceans. Some are removed, some are recycled but at present the total volume is accumulating At sea we can begin to capture them with seaweed farms. On land, we clearly have to improve our capacity to recover plastics especially the microplastics.

A Business Model To Solve Plastic Pollution

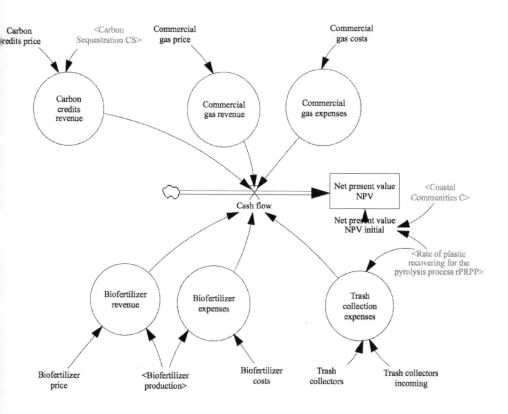

The combination of pyrolysis and digester technologies leads to a business model with multiple cash flows. The revenue streams include: carbon credits, gas sales, subsidy savings (for governments), fertilizer sales and savings through replacement of chemical fertilizers with bio fertilizers, and trash collection savings for governments through the plastic cleanup campaigns. The increase in cash flow and benefits for society lift the value of the assets both in private and public ownership. This has a multiplier effect and strengthens the resilience of the society over time, readying it for hard times (which will always come).

About the authors

Gunter Pauli (1956) is an established author who published his first books in 1987. His latest sequel of three editions of *The Blue Economy* has been translated into 43 languages and has reached over a million readers. Pauli is an entrepreneur who embraces groundbreaking and pioneering initiatives. He is dedicated to the transformation of society, designs a fundamentally new business model, and goes out of his way to turn vision into reality. Pauli witnessed, learned from, pushed forward, and/or started up over 200 projects in every corner of the world. He has also written about 280 fables to educate and inspire children about how nature works.

Marco Simeoni (1966) grew up in the Lausanne region in French-speaking Switzerland before studying engineering. An entrepreneur as well as an engineer, he created the IT consultancy firm Veltigroup, the largest not listed on the stock exchange IT provider in Switzerland. In 2010, Marco utilised his passion for the oceans and his expertise as an engineer-entrepreneur to found the Race for Water Foundation. "I've always been passionate about sailing and the oceans. I couldn't stand by watching them deteriorate and do nothing".

Jurriaan Kamp (1959) is founder and curator of the "solutions news" platform, KAMP SOLUTIONS. In 1995, he left a successful career as the chief economics editor at the leading Dutch newspaper, *NRC Handelsblad*, to co-found the "solutions journalism" magazine *Ode* in the Netherlands. In 2004, he moved to California and launched the international edition of the magazine, renamed *The Intelligent Optimist* in 2012. In 2015, Kamp launched a daily online solutions news service, *The Optimist Daily*. He has since moved on launching KAMP SOLUTIONS. Kamp is the author of several books and has regularly come in ahead of the curve on stories that advance new visions for our world.

Made in the USA
San Bernardino, CA
17 July 2020

75662945R00097